THE SHAKER KITCHEN

JEFFREY S. PAIGE

The

CLARKSON POTTER/PUBLISHERS
NEW YORK

OVER 100 RECIPES
FROM CANTERBURY
SHAKER VILLAGE

Shaker Kitchen

In memory of Eldress Bertha Lindsay
and Sister Ethel Hudson,
who took me into their hearts and kitchen,
and shared with me their love and
appreciation for good food.

Grateful acknowledgment is made to the following for permission to reprint
previously published material:

THE COUNTRYMAN PRESS, INC.: recipes from *Seasoned With Grace*
by Eldress Bertha Lindsay. Copyright © 1987 by The Shaker Village, Inc.,
Canterbury, N.H. Reprinted by permission of The Countryman Press, Inc.
MACMILLAN PUBLISHING COMPANY: recipes from *The Best of*
Shaker Cooking by Amy Bess Miller and Persis Fuller. Copyright © 1970 by Shaker
Communities, Inc. Copyright © 1985 by Amy Bess Miller. Reprinted by permission of
Macmillan Publishing Company.
RODALE PRESS: recipes from *Cooking in the Shaker Spirit* by James
Haller and Jeffrey Paige. Copyright © 1990 by James Haller and Jeffrey
Paige. Reprinted by permission of Rodale Press, Inc.;
Emmaus, Penn. 18098.
Some recipes in this book may have originally appeared in slightly different form in
The Union Leader Corp. publications.

Published by Clarkson N. Potter Inc., 201 East 50th Street, New York, New York
10022. Member of the Crown Publishing Group.

Random House, Inc., New York, Toronto, London, Sydney, Auckland

CLARKSON N. POTTER, POTTER, and colophon are trademarks of
Clarkson N. Potter, Inc.

Manufactured in the United States of America
DESIGN BY GINA DAVIS
Library of Congress Cataloging-in-Publication Data

Paige, Jeffrey, 1964–
The Shaker kitchen: Over 100 recipes from Canterbury Shaker Village /
Jeffrey S. Paige.—1st ed.
Includes bibliographical references.
1. Cookery, Shaker.   2. Shakers—New Hampshire—Canterbury.   3. Creamery
(Restaurant: Canterbury, N.H.)
4. Shaker Village, Inc.   I. Shaker Village, Inc.   II. Title.
TX715.P155   1994

641.5'088288—dc20   93-2360
CIP

ISBN 0-517-58838-2
10   9   8   7   6   5   4   3   2   1
First Edition

ACKNOWLEDGMENTS

I began working on this book in the summer of 1988, and over the past six years many people have contributed in one way or another in aiding in its completion. *The Shaker Kitchen* has been not only a dream of mine but one shared by my family, friends, and the many people who dine at The Creamery and visit the Canterbury Shaker Village Museum annually. I'd like to take this opportunity to express my sincere gratitude and extend a heart-felt "thank you" to:

Betty and Ken Paige, my parents, for always allowing me and encouraging me to be me. I couldn't have made it this far without you.

Bud and Darryl Thompson, for sharing their knowledge, time, and friendship.

Jim Haller, who encouraged me to cook for myself and to never be afraid in the kitchen.

Jasper White, who instilled in me a deep sense of pride and respect for New England's rich culinary heritage.

Tim McTague, for his friendship and unique sense of humor that helped me get through it all. And, I almost forgot, for his dedication to providing the best-quality stone-ground flours in the good old U.S.A.

George Covey, Wade Bennett, Bill Vinal, Ted Colby, Justin Despres, Louise Moore, Pat Messier, Michelle York, Mary Jane Moulton, Terry Flaherty, Cindy Moore, Marge Ennis, Joyce Terrill, Glenda Yeaton, Emily Johnson, René Paguette, and Renée

Fox, the staff, past and present, of The Creamery who keeps the spirit of the Canterbury Shakers' love for good food alive.

Dan Holmes, Ken Ryan, and Eero Ruuttila for providing all those wonderful organic veggies.

Jessica Stebbins, Karen and Jamie Soucy, Keith Nelson, Bob Nolan, Jane Beck, Leslie Miller, Ellie Ferriter, Mary Holland, Brian Urkevic, and Jacque and Paula Despres for their assistance, constant support, and friendship.

Katie Workman, my editor, and the staff at Clarkson Potter for capturing the Shaker spirit.

Meg Ruley, my agent for believing in this project as much as I did.

Ken Haedrich, for sharing his agent with a fellow New Hampshire cook.

CONTENTS

*T*ESTIMONIAL

WHILE THE SHAKERS ARE PARTICULARLY FAMOUS FOR BEAUTIFUL and simple furniture, equal attention should be given to our cooking. There is something to the axiom that cooks are born, not made. Although I believe that all people can learn to cook and prepare a good meal, natural ability allows a person to give extra attention to whatever is made. Indeed, cooking is an art just as much as painting a picture or making a piece of furniture. For if a meal is prepared with fine produce, the natural cook knows how to give it the special touch, not only making it eye-appealing, but also delicious.

For the past three seasons, Jeffrey Paige has been our chef at The Creamery, Canterbury Shaker Village's restaurant. To me Jeffrey is a master chef, as he needs no assistance in planning, cooking, and serving a meal. A good chef knows the value of having a dish taste as good as it looks. Jeffrey has certainly achieved the height of master cooking, as his dishes are well planned, taste good, and are eye-appealing as I like.

I have long been a devotee of fine cooking, and while I'm not a master chef myself, I can certainly give credit to Jeffrey as being one of the world's best chefs today.

E LDRESS B ERTHA L INDSAY
Canterbury Shaker Village
August 1990

FOREWORD

THE SHAKERS: A LEGACY OF STEWARDSHIP

By Darryl Thompson

I cannot speak for the Shakers, but I can speak of them. I am not a Shaker and yet have lived among them part-time and full-time for nearly all my life. My credentials are not those of a spokesman with authority to speak on behalf of the Shaker Society: the Shakers have spoken for themselves—clearly and eloquently—for over two hundred years. Rather, my testimony is that of a witness. I speak from the standpoint of personal experience, as someone who has loved them profoundly and known them in the varied roles of employers, friends, and "adopted family."

People have sometimes asked me to give them a concise definition of Shaker beliefs. That is difficult to some extent because Shakerism is better defined as a life-style based on certain fundamental values and beliefs than as a theological "system." Its spirit is something so powerful and deep that it shatters the narrow restrictions of classification, so yeasty and effervescent that it easily overflows any definitive mold into which someone attempts to pour it.

Books are certainly an indispensable asset in any quest to know the Shakers. But they are only entranceways into a reality that must be experientially known. Emily Dickinson once said that biographies can only contain the fragrance of an individual life but not the life itself. The same thing can be said about books that recount the biography of a people. From books you can learn the basic facts: that the first Shakers—a band of nine including their inspired leader Mother Ann Lee—first touched American shores in 1774; that in England they had grown out of the little group of religious dissenters who had met in the home of James and Jane Wardley, Quaker tailors living in the area of Manchester; that the Wardley group (or "Shaking Quakers" as they were called due to the physical manifestations produced by the experience of being filled with the Spirit in their meetings) melded together the influences of Quakerism, of the French Prophets (or "Camisards") and their English followers, and perhaps of George Whitefield and the Wesleys[1]; that Ann Lee joined the Wardley society about 1758[2] and the passage of time and events gradually led the Wardleys to turn over the group's leadership to her. But these are only "the facts, not the phosphorescence" (to again borrow a phrase from Dickinson).

If you would truly know the Shakers, I would recommend scanning an old document recording amounts of food, clothing, and money that the Shakers distributed to the poor; or hearing the firsthand account of an orphan who was given love, discipline, vocational training, and an education by a caring Shaker community; or—if at all possible—talking to living Shakers. It would also be my suggestion that you trace your hand along the smooth, sinuous curve of a staircase banister in an old Shaker house or sit in quiet contemplation of the elegant simplicity of a Shaker candlestand—all part of a magnificent craft heritage that has enriched contemporary craftsmanship, influenced modern design in both Scandinavia and the United States, and spawned an entire industry of craftspeople making "reproduction Shaker" or "Shaker-inspired" furniture and objects. Furthermore, I would encourage you to sample the unique taste of an apple pie flavored with rosewater, another product of a group that made some valuable contributions to the art and science of cookery. While you are at it, listen to a few of the more than ten thousand songs that the Believers authored (in some cases creating both the words and the music and in other instances "redeeming" tunes borrowed from "the world" by fitting them with new words expressing the faith of the church), a legacy of song and dance that at least a few twentieth-century songwriters, composers, and choreographers have drawn upon as a resource. It would also be helpful to investigate how the outside world's artists and writers have found inspiration or source material in Shaker culture.

Also don't forget to smell the savory scent of drying herbs or to

---

1. Edward Deming Andrews, *The People Called Shakers* (New York: Dover Publications, Inc., 1963), pp. 5–7.
2. Andrews, *The People Called Shakers*, p. 5.

examine the results of Shaker gardening expertise, for it was as horticulturists that the Shakers achieved some of their most important accomplishments. They were the first in the United States to sell garden seeds in paper packages and, as major seed suppliers and among the nation's earliest seedsmen, they had a significant impact on the variety and quality of crops grown by American farmers. They are considered to have been the first in the country to sell medicinal herbs and herbal medicines on a large commercial scale, thus greatly aiding the development of that industry in the United States.

I would also urge you to plan a tour of the nation's Shaker museums and learn something about the Order's contributions to technological invention and improvement. The Covenant, the remarkable document which is to Shaker government what the U.S. Constitution is to American democracy, speaks of the necessity of improving time as well as talents. Herein is one of the prime reasons that the Shakers developed so many laborsaving devices. Time belonged to God and man was accountable for how he spent it. Time saved by inventions and improvements could be better used in other ways—in worship, in performing other kinds of labor, in study or helping the poor. A partial list of Shaker inventions and improvements (and I emphasize its incompleteness) includes a dough-kneading machine, a cream separator, a washing machine, a "land leveler," a chimney cap, the first circular saw in the United States, a method of making false teeth, a screw propeller, a turbine water-wheel, a vertical saw with an attached device for cleaning the saw blade by means of compressed air, a machine for making tongue and groove boards, a water-powered wind fan, a fly trap, a musical instrument called the "piano-violin," "hair caps" for balding brethren, a hernia truss, a cultivator, a metal ball-and-socket "tilter" for chairs, a cast-iron fence post, a type of plough, a lathe, a Shaker sash balance and lock, a pea sheller, and the vacuum pan that Gail Borden, an acquaintance of the Mount Lebanon Shakers, used to invent condensed milk.[3]

Lastly, I would urge you to talk to scholars who have specialized in researching some particular category of Shaker contributions, for the Shakers' influence was also felt in such diverse fields as industry, animal husbandry, architecture, folk art, religious life and thought, social reform, racial equality, women's rights, and communitarian history.

The New Jerusalem Bible renders the question in Luke 12:42 as, "Who, then, is the wise and trustworthy steward whom the master will place over his household to give them at the proper time their allowance of food?" For over two centuries the Shakers have proven themselves collectively to be wise and trustworthy stewards of the Master, standing ready to serve Him with love, faith, and total consecration, prepared to serve their fellow men and women with caring, wisdom, and creativity.

May we learn not only from the wonderful food traditions they have given us, but also from the spiritual philosophy of stewardship that is their even greater gift to the nation and the world.

---

3. Perhaps the best list of Shaker inventions (although not a complete list) is found on pp. 152–59 of *Work and Worship: The Economic Order of The Shakers* by Edward Deming Andrews and Faith Andrews (Greenwich, Conn.: New York Graphic Society, 1974). Also see the pamphlet *Consecrated Ingenuity: The Shakers and Their Inventions* by John S. Williams (Old Chatham, N.Y.: The Shaker Museum Foundation, 1957). The water-powered wind fan appears as one of June Sprigg's exquisite drawings on p. 122 of *By Shaker Hands* [(written and illustrated by June Sprigg) (New York: Alfred Knopf, 1975)]. The fly trap, "piano-violin," and several other ingenious devices are covered in the section on Elisha D'Alembert Blakeman in *Shaker Furniture Makers* by Jerry V. Grant and Douglas R. Allen (Hanover, N.H. and London: Published by University Press of New England for Hancock Shaker Village, Inc., of Pittsfield, Massachusetts, 1990).

INTRODUCTION

Perhaps the most important aspect of Shaker cuisine is its attitude toward food and its preparation. In Shaker kitchens meals were planned and cooked to satisfy both bodily and, in a sense, spiritual hunger. The Sisters prepared food as efficiently, nutritiously, and tastily as possible. They steamed vegetables to retain nutrients and saved parings and leftovers for their "pot licker" soups. They knew, too, that meals must "create contentment, joy, and satisfaction in those who partake of them." In this respect, herbs became almost a necessity to the Shakers' simple fare because they were a means of making each dish "a fascinating, outstanding viand."

The contents of this book are not merely a collection of photos and food but rather a treasure chest of memories, experiences, and influences my dear friends, the Canterbury Shakers, have given me to cherish for the rest of my life.

To understand our Shaker-inspired cooking one must first understand the Shakers and their mission in forming a utopian society in the eighteenth and nineteenth centuries. The Shakers were a religious group dedicated to "creating a heaven on earth." They worked with the same dedication and sense of purpose in their kitchens as they did in the fields, workshops, and their house of worship.

Like their furniture and architecture, aspects of Shakerism with which most of us are familiar, their cooking was simple and unadulterated. Their meals made the most of seasonal ingredients, more often then not grown and raised at the Village. Dishes like Fish Chowder with Whipped Cream Biscuits and Baked Country

Smoked Ham with Spiced Cherry Catsup are as welcome to Village visitors today as they were to hungry Brethren and Sisters over 150 years ago.

Today at The Creamery restaurant, our menus are a blend of "something old and something new." With Eldress Bertha's words of wisdom to guide us, "take the ordinary and make it extraordinary in everything you do," the kitchen staff has become dedicated to preparing dishes without compromise. Using the highest quality local purveyors—smokehouses, gristmills, family-owned farms and Village-raised fruits, vegetables, and herbs for a solid foundation— we're able to keep the Shaker spirit alive in the kitchen and offer a true taste of the country.

I'm grateful for the opportunity to share my experiences and knowledge, as the last cook to train under the Canterbury Shakers, who so kindly and lovingly shared with me. If I may leave you with just one parting thought that summarizes my approach to food and cooking, it is this quote from Shaker Kitchen Sister Lisset: "No cook is really good without a lively imagination and the will to use it."

Here's to a little fun in the kitchen.

SOUPS AND CHOWDERS

CHILLED MINTED STRAWBERRY YOGURT SOUP

For years the Canterbury Shakers relished their indigenous wild strawberries, which are smaller and sweeter than their cultivated counterparts. Unfortunately most strawberries available today are of the cultivated variety, but it is worth seeking out the wild berries for this refreshing soup.

This soup is the perfect beginning for a light spring lunch and often completes a hot summer night's dinner at The Creamery.

1 cup loosely packed spearmint leaves, washed	1 quart natural plain yogurt
1 cup sugar	Plain yogurt, sliced strawberries, and spearmint leaves to garnish
2 pints fresh strawberries, washed and hulled	
¾ cup honey	

1. Combine the mint and sugar in the bowl of a food processor, and process until the mint is finely minced. Add the strawberries and honey, and process until the berries are pureed.

2. In a large bowl, combine the strawberry puree with the yogurt, and stir until well blended. Cover and refrigerate the soup overnight.

3. Ladle the soup into bowls and serve cold, garnished with a dollop of yogurt, a strawberry slice, and a fresh spearmint leaf.

SERVES 6 TO 8

CRANBERRY BEAN SOUP

This is a very hearty soup that finds its way to the dinner table when fresh apple cider is in season. It's a meal all unto itself, needing only some hot buttered biscuits to make it complete.

The recipe calls for cranberry beans, also known as shell beans or succotash beans, which the Shakers grew in quantity, as they could be dried and used all year long. However, just about any bean will do; or try a combination of two or three different beans.

2 cups dried cranberry
   beans
1 tablespoon finely
   chopped garlic
2 medium onions, peeled
   and diced
1 cup sliced and washed
   leeks
2 cups diced carrots
1 pound smoked sausage,
   such as kielbasa, diced

1 quart apple cider, plus
   more as needed
1 quart beef or chicken
   stock, plus more as
   needed
2 tablespoons chopped
   fresh parsley
2 teaspoons minced fresh
   thyme
Salt and freshly ground
   pepper to taste

1. Pick through the beans and rinse under cold water. Soak the beans overnight in enough water to cover them. Drain.

2. In a large soup pot, combine all of the ingredients except the salt and pepper. Heat to a boil over medium heat and simmer for 2½ to 3 hours, or until the beans are soft, adding more cider and stock if needed. Season with salt and pepper, and serve.

SERVES 6 TO 8

FRESH HERBAL BROTH WITH SHAKER DROP DUMPLINGS

Since the Shakers were the first to commercially cultivate and package garden seeds, and ran an extensive dried herb industry, it's only natural that we include this simple recipe for Shaker herbal broth.

Shaker Drop Dumplings (recipe follows)	**1 tablespoon chopped fresh tarragon**
2 quarts beef or chicken stock	**2 tablespoons chopped fresh celery leaves**
2 tablespoons chopped fresh parsley	**1 tablespoon chopped fresh basil**
2 tablespoons chopped fresh sorrel	**3 bay leaves**
	Salt and freshly ground pepper to taste

1. Prepare the batter for the drop dumplings.

2. In a large soup pot, combine the stock, parsley, sorrel, tarragon, celery leaves, basil, and bay leaves. Bring the seasoned broth to a boil over medium heat, then lower the heat to a simmer and cook for 15 to 20 minutes. Remove the bay leaves.

3. Place a colander over the soup pot. Pour the dumpling batter into the colander, and using a spatula, push the batter through the colander into the broth. Stir the soup immediately to prevent the dumplings from sticking together. Season the soup with salt and pepper, and serve hot.

SERVES 6 TO 8

VARIATION

Two cups of cooked rice may be substituted for the dumplings.

SHAKER HERB GARDENS One of the biggest thrills of being the chef at the Creamery is the abundance of fresh ingredients grown on the property. In keeping with the Shakers' two hundred-year-old tradition of harvesting and drying herbs, Heidi Herzberger and a group of highly dedicated volunteers tend to the Village's herb terraces. They plant, care for, harvest, dry, and package authentic culinary herb mixes, four mint teas, and a moth repellent. I enjoy the large variety of fresh herbs grown each season: mints, basil, tarragon, thyme, summer savory, parsley, chives, sage, oregano, rosemary, just to name a few. Herbs are an important part of our Shaker-inspired cooking. There's really no substitute for that fresh-picked taste.

S HAKER   D ROP   D UMPLINGS

2 large eggs	**1 teaspoon chopped fresh**
½ cup milk	**parsley**
1½ cups unbleached all-	**Pinch of salt**
purpose flour	**Pinch of freshly ground**
	pepper

1. In a blender or bowl, combine the eggs and milk, and mix well.

2. In a medium-sized bowl, combine the flour, parsley, salt, and pepper, then stir in the milk mixture to form a smooth batter. Cover and allow the batter to rest for at least 15 minutes before using.

MAKES ABOUT 2 CUPS OF BATTER

HOW TO TELL A
GOOD POTATO

Here is a good place in which to impart what is a secret to the vast majority of people, and it is one well worth knowing. It is simple how to tell a good potato; that is, as well as it can be done without cooking it, for sometimes even experts are deceived. Take a sound potato, and paying no attention to its outward appearance, divide it into two pieces with your knife and examine the exposed surfaces. If there is so much water or "juice" that seemingly a slight pressure would cause it to fall off in drops, you may be sure it will be "soggy" after it is boiled. These are the requisite qualities for a good potato, which must appear when one is cut in two: For color, a yellowish white; if it is a deep yellow the potato will not cook well; there must be a considerable amount of moisture, though not too much; rub the two pieces together and a white froth will appear around the edges and upon the two surfaces; this signifies the presence of starch, and the more starch, and consequently froth, the better the potato, while the less there is the poorer it will cook. The strength of the starchy element can be tested by releasing the hold upon one piece of the potato, and if it still clings to the other, this in itself is a very good sign. These are the experiments generally made by experts, and they are ordinarily willing to buy on the strength of their turning out well, though, as stated above, these tests are by no means infallible.

THE SHAKER MANIFESTO   OCTOBER 1881

FOUR ONION AND NEW POTATO CREAM SOUP

This is one of those soups that can be served pretty much year-round. In the summer we serve it chilled and during the winter months piping hot.

The recipe calls for four different kind of onions, and you should feel free to experiment and substitute whatever varieties you might have on hand, as the Shakers did. Each onion brings its unique taste and character to the soup.

½ cup (1 stick) unsalted
    butter
2 medium onions, peeled
    and thinly sliced
2 cups sliced and washed
    leeks
½ cup minced shallots
1 pound red potatoes,
    scrubbed

About 5 to 6 cups chicken
    stock, or to cover
1 cup light cream
1 cup heavy cream
½ cup sliced scallions,
    including greens
Salt and freshly ground
    pepper to taste

1. In a large soup pot, melt the butter over medium heat. Add the onions, leeks, and shallots and cook until the onions are lightly browned, about 7 to 10 minutes, stirring often.

2. Meanwhile, quarter and slice the potatoes by hand or in a food processor, about ¼ inch thick. Add these to the soup pot and add enough chicken stock to cover the potatoes and onions. Heat the soup to a boil over medium heat, then reduce the heat to a simmer and cook 15 minutes, or until the potatoes are just tender. Carefully remove 2 to 3 cups of the soup with some vegetables, puree in a blender or food processor, and then return to the soup pot.

3. To serve the soup chilled, remove from the heat and cool the soup base completely. Refrigerate until cold. Stir in the light and heavy cream and the scallions, and season with salt and pepper. Serve cold. To serve the soup hot, add the light and heavy cream and the scallions, and season with salt and pepper. Cook gently until heated through and serve hot.

SERVES 6 TO 8

BAKED ONION AND APPLE CIDER SOUP WITH SMOKED CHEDDAR CHEESE

Caramelized onions simmered in fresh local cider and then baked under smoked Vermont Cheddar cheese make this the most popular soup on our winter menus. I don't know of a better way to warm up on a blisteringly cold winter night.

½ cup (1 stick) unsalted butter

5 medium onions, peeled and thinly sliced

4 cups beef stock

4 cups fresh apple cider

2 teaspoons minced fresh thyme

¼ cup light brown sugar (omit if cider is sweet enough)

Salt and freshly ground pepper to taste

Butter as needed for spreading

6 to 8 slices of French bread, cut ¼ inch thick

6 to 8 thin (⅛ inch) slices of Gruyère cheese

3 to 4 cups grated smoked Cheddar cheese

1. In a large soup pot, melt the butter over medium-low heat. Add the onions and cook until well browned, about 15 minutes, taking care not to burn them. Add the stock, cider, and thyme, bring the soup to a boil, then lower the heat and simmer the soup for 1½ hours. Skim the top of the soup periodically.

2. Season the soup with the brown sugar, if needed, and salt and pepper. The soup may be made up to this point a day ahead and kept covered in the refrigerator.

3. Preheat the oven to 400°F. Put 6 to 8 ovenproof soup crocks in a large roasting pan and fill the crocks with the hot soup. Pour hot water into the roasting pan to come halfway up the sides of the crocks.

4. To make the croutons, lightly butter the slices of French bread and broil until lightly browned on both sides.

5. Top each crock of soup with a crouton, a slice of Gruyère cheese, and ⅓ to ½ cup grated smoked Cheddar cheese. Bake the soup until the cheese is lightly golden brown and the soup is hot and bubbly. Serve immediately.

SERVES 6 TO 8

RADISH CREAM SOUP WITH FRESH DILL

½ cup (1 stick) unsalted
 butter
1 medium onion, peeled
 and diced
4 cups trimmed, cleaned,
 and thinly sliced red
 radishes
2 tablespoons minced fresh
 dill

½ cup unbleached
 all-purpose flour
4 cups chicken stock
1 cup heavy cream
1 cup light cream
Salt and freshly ground
 pepper to taste
Fresh dill to garnish

1. In a large soup pot, melt the butter over low heat. Add the onion, radishes, and dill, and cook until the vegetables are translucent, about 5 to 7 minutes, stirring often. Stir in the flour and cook for 2 to 3 minutes, not allowing to color, stirring often. Stir in the chicken stock until smooth and simmer the soup over medium heat, about 15 to 20 minutes, or until the vegetables are tender. Stir often.

2. Carefully puree the soup in batches in a blender or food processor, then return to the soup pot.

3. Stir in the heavy and light cream, and season with salt and pepper. Heat the soup to just below a simmer, but do not allow it to come to a boil. Ladle the soup into bowls, and garnish with a sprig of fresh dill.

SERVES 6 TO 8

Traditional Corn Chowder with Five Variations

This is the basic recipe and method of preparation I use to create a number of wonderful corn-based chowders. By simply changing one or two ingredients, you can create a new and exciting dish, as the Sisters did using the various ingredients that found their way into the kitchen. This is a perfect example of how through their economical-mindedness they concocted wonderful dishes simply by using the leftovers at hand.

The five recipes that follow are just a sampling of the variations on corn chowder we serve at The Creamery.

½ pound smoked slab
    bacon, diced
1½ pounds red potatoes,
    scrubbed
1 medium onion, peeled
    and diced
2 bay leaves
4 to 5 cups chicken stock,
    or to cover

3 cups corn kernels,
    preferably fresh
2 tablespoons chopped
    fresh parsley
1 cup heavy cream
Salt and freshly ground
    pepper to taste

1. In a large soup pot, fry the bacon over medium heat just until it starts to crisp, about 8 to 10 minutes.

2. Meanwhile, quarter and slice the potatoes by hand or in a food processor, about ¼ inch thick. Set aside.

3. Add the onion and bay leaves to the bacon, and cook until the onion is translucent, about 3 to 5 minutes. Carefully drain off half of the bacon grease and discard.

4. Add the potatoes to the soup pot, add enough stock to cover the potatoes, and bring to a simmer over medium heat. Simmer until the potatoes are tender, about 15 minutes. Add the corn, parsley, and cream, and cook until heated through, stirring often. Remove the bay leaves. Season with salt and pepper, and serve.

SERVES 6 TO 8

NOTE: To thicken the chowder slightly, dissolve ¼ cup flour in ½ cup cold water. Stir this into the chowder just before adding the corn.

ABOUT "SUNDAY CORN"

A man out west recently boasted that his two acres of "Sunday corn," on which all the work had been done on Sunday and which yielded seventy bushels to the acre, upset the Bible idea that Sunday work never prospers. To this the editor of an agricultural paper replied thus: "If the author of this shallow nonsense had read the Bible half as much as he has the works of its opponents, he would have known that the great Ruler of the universe does not always square up his accounts with man-kind in the month of October."

THE SHAKER MANIFESTO   JANUARY 1879

VARIATIONS

SWEET POTATO CORN CHOWDER

Add 1 large sweet potato, peeled and diced, and ¼ cup light brown sugar along with the potatoes and stock.

NATIVE CORN AND PUMPKIN CHOWDER

Stir in 2 cups pumpkin puree, ½ cup sliced scallions, ¼ cup light brown sugar, and ½ teaspoon ground cinnamon when the corn, parsley, and cream are added to the soup.

NATIVE CORN AND LOBSTER CHOWDER

If possible, substitute lobster stock for the chicken stock. Reduce the amount of corn from 3 to 2 cups and add 2 cups chopped cooked lobster meat, and 2 tablespoons minced fresh chives when the corn, parsley, and cream are added to the soup.

BUTTERNUT SQUASH AND CORN CHOWDER

Add 2 cups peeled and diced butternut (or delicata, blue Hubbard, buttercup, or acorn) squash along with the potatoes and stock. Stir in ¼ cup light brown sugar and ½ cup sliced scallions, including greens, when the corn, parsley and cream are added to the soup.

FISH CHOWDER WITH TOASTED COMMON CRACKERS

New Englanders love a good, hearty bowl of fish chowder and the Canterbury Shakers were no exception. If you can't find common crackers, serve the chowder with hot buttered Whipped Cream Biscuits (page 40).

½ pound smoked slab bacon, cut into medium dice (see Sources)
1½ pounds red potatoes, scrubbed
1 medium onion, peeled and diced
2 bay leaves
4 to 5 cups fish or chicken stock, or to cover

1½ pounds boneless and skinless white fish fillets, cut into large dice
2 tablespoons chopped fresh parsley
2 cups heavy cream
Salt and freshly ground pepper to taste
8 to 10 common crackers
Butter for spreading

1. In a large soup pot, fry the bacon over medium heat just until it starts to crisp, about 8 to 10 minutes. Meanwhile, quarter and slice the potatoes by hand or in a food processor, about ¼ inch thick. Set aside.

2. Add the onion and bay leaves to the bacon, and cook, stirring occasionally, until the onion is translucent, about 3 to 5 minutes. Carefully drain off half of the bacon grease and discard. Add the potatoes to the soup pot, add enough stock to cover the potatoes, and bring to a simmer over medium heat. Simmer until the potatoes are tender, about 15 minutes.

3. Add the fish and parsley, and simmer until the fish is cooked, about 5 minutes (see Note) Stir in the heavy cream, season with salt and pepper, and serve the hot chowder in bowls.

TO TOAST THE COMMON CRACKERS

4. Split the crackers in half with a fork. Lightly butter each half and toast under a broiler until lightly browned. Serve warm.

SERVES 6 TO 8

NOTE: To thicken the chowder slightly, dissolve ¼ cup unbleached all-purpose flour in ½ cup cold water. Stir this into the chowder just before you add the fish.

SMOKED MAINE SHRIMP BISQUE

Maine shrimp are probably the last great gift of the ocean that have yet to be discovered by non-New Englanders, and most New Englanders for that matter. Available basically in the winter months, December to March, these tiny, sweet coastal shrimp, (sixty to seventy-five to the pound) are sold cheaply all along the roadsides of Maine and New Hampshire.

This soup uses a combination of both fresh and smoked Maine shrimp, which are not so cheap, to produce its rich, delicate flavor. If you can't find Maine shrimp you can substitute any shrimp, fresh or frozen. You'll just have to plan a trip to New England to see what you've been missing.

3 tablespoons unsalted
butter

2 tablespoons minced fresh
shallots

1 teaspoon finely chopped
garlic

1 pound peeled fresh
Maine shrimp

3 tablespoons unbleached
all-purpose flour

2 cups shrimp, fish, or
chicken stock

1 pound smoked Maine
shrimp (see Sources)

1 tablespoon chopped
fresh parsley

1 cup light cream

Salt and freshly ground
pepper to taste

1. In a large soup pot, melt the butter over medium-low heat. Add the shallots and garlic, and cook just until aromatic, about 1 minute. Add the fresh shrimp and cook for 2 to 3 minutes, stirring often. Stir in the flour and cook for 2 to 3 minutes, stirring often, but not allowing to color. Stir in the stock until smooth. Simmer over medium heat until the soup thickens, about 6 to 8 minutes, stirring often.

2. Add the smoked shrimp and carefully puree the soup in batches in a blender or food processor. Return to the soup pot. Add the parsley and cream, and season with salt and pepper. Cook, stirring, until heated through, and serve.

SERVES 4 TO 6

SHAKER KITCHEN INVENTIONS Unlike their good friends the Amish, the Shakers embraced modern technology and always strove to make everyday life simpler for themselves in all aspects. There is no better testament to this than their kitchen inventions. Ongoing research is continually bringing to light their many ingenious devices, and the following have all been confirmed as authentic Shaker designs:

- Hand-cranked dough kneading machine: expended less energy
- Motorized ice cream freezer: also less work
- Apple peeler: faster than by hand
- Apple corer and slicer: made the ubiquitous pies and applesauce much easier
- Cream separator: easily separated milk and cream
- Corn sheller for dried corn: kernels were used in everything from cooking to feeding the farm animals
- Double roller rolling pin: two pins flattened the dough at once, cutting the rolling time down
- Flat corn broom: replaced the unevenly bristled broom, covering more surface area of the floor

The Shakers baking oven is still in the bake room of the Canterbury Village today. It's a huge contraption, sporting four doors on the front, each opening to a four-foot round metal plate on a post that you can rotate to make it easier to fill the large oven space with food, and also to facilitate more even cooking.

Next to the oven are the arch kettles, big kettles sunk into a brick foundation with a fire underneath.

My friend and mentor James Haller always said, "If you take the drudgery out of the kitchen and fill it with the light of possibility, you can adopt excellence as your tradition and be bound only by the production of quality." After knowing the Canterbury Shakers for over twenty years, I think a little has rubbed off on him and I am grateful to have worked with him so a little could rub off on me.

SALADS AND DRESSINGS

WARM FIDDLEHEAD FERN POTATO SALAD

This is a German-style potato salad that is prepared in and served directly from the frying pan. I serve this during the month of May when local fiddleheads are in season. However, I've found that this method of preparation works equally well with artichoke hearts, broccoli, and asparagus tips during other seasons. This recipe is adapted from one I found in an old Shaker cookbook.

2 pounds red potatoes, scrubbed
2 cups fiddlehead ferns, washed and trimmed
4 tablespoons (½ stick) unsalted butter
1 medium onion, peeled and thinly sliced
1 cup crumbled cooked bacon

2 tablespoons cider vinegar
1 to 2 tablespoons sugar
2 tablespoons chopped fresh parsley
Salt and freshly ground pepper to taste

1. Fill a large saucepan half full with water and add a table-spoon of salt. Bring to a boil over medium heat. Add the potatoes and cook for 15 to 20 minutes, until cooked through but still very firm when pierced with a knife. Drain well and cut into ¼-inch-thick slices.

2. Fill a medium saucepan half full with water and a couple of pinches of salt. Bring to a boil over medium heat. Add the fiddleheads and cook for 1 minute, then drain and rinse imme-diately with cold water. Drain again and set aside.

3. In a large frying pan, melt the butter over medium heat, add the onion, and cook, stirring, until translucent, 3 to 5 min-utes. Increase the heat to medium-high and add the sliced pota-toes, blanched fiddlehead ferns, and cooked bacon, and sauté for 2 to 3 minutes, tossing often. Add the vinegar, 1 tablespoon sugar, and parsley. Toss gently and continue to cook another minute or so.

4. Season with salt, freshly ground pepper, and more sugar, if necessary, to taste. Serve warm.

SERVES 6 TO 8

BLUEBERRY LAVENDER VINAIGRETTE

Ella Eleanor "Mildred" Wells was the inspiration for this unique and most sought-after salad dressing at The Creamery. She lived with the Canterbury Shakers almost her entire life and loved to cook and garden. Framing the entranceway to her living quarters are two beautiful lavender patches. The patches date back over ninety years and were the focus of my cooking for one entire spring. There's something about the combination of fresh lavender and wild blueberries. . . . I'll let the vinaigrette speak for itself. This is delicious on tossed salads with a combination of lettuces.

2 cups fresh wild blueberries, washed and picked over

1 teaspoon lavender blossoms, washed

¼ cup maple syrup, preferably dark amber or grade B

3 cups vegetable oil

1 cup blueberry lavender vinegar (see Sources) or white vinegar

2 tablespoons Dijon mustard, or more as needed

3 tablespoons sugar, or more as needed

1. In a large saucepan, stir the blueberries, lavender blossoms, and maple syrup over medium heat until the berries burst, about 3 to 5 minutes. Cook for 5 minutes longer, stirring frequently. Remove the saucepan from the heat and cool the mixture completely.

2. In a food processor or blender, combine the cooled blueberry mixture, vegetable oil, vinegar, mustard, and sugar, and process for 5 to 8 seconds. Add a little more mustard to emulsify the vinaigrette, if necessary. Add additional sugar to taste, if necessary. Refrigerate the dressing, covered, for at least 2 hours before serving.

MAKES APPROXIMATELY 4 CUPS

CHILLED FIDDLEHEAD, POTATO, AND EGG SALAD

In addition to often eating lunch in the fields on workdays, the Shakers loved a good picnic. This is a traditional backyard barbecue potato egg salad with the addition of fiddlehead ferns. If fiddleheads are unavailable or out of season, just omit them.

¾ cup mayonnaise
¾ cup sour cream
2 tablespoons cider
  vinegar
1 tablespoon Dijon
  mustard

2 teaspoons finely chopped
  garlic
1 tablespoon honey
1 tablespoon chopped
  fresh parsley

2 pounds Maine or red
  potatoes, scrubbed
2 cups fiddlehead ferns,
  washed and trimmed
¼ cup diced red onion

4 hard-cooked eggs,
  peeled and chopped
Salt and freshly ground
  pepper to taste

TO MAKE THE DRESSING

1. In a large bowl, combine the mayonnaise, sour cream, vinegar, mustard, garlic, honey, and parsley, and mix well. Cover and refrigerate until needed, up to one day ahead.

TO MAKE THE SALAD

2. Fill a large saucepan half full with water and add a tablespoon of salt. Bring to a boil over medium heat. Add the potatoes and cook for 30 minutes, or until the potatoes are tender when pierced with a knife. Drain and cool. When the potatoes are cool enough to handle, peel and then cut them into 1-inch cubes.

3. Fill a medium saucepan half full with water and add a couple of pinches of salt. Heat to a boil over medium heat. Add the fiddleheads and cook for 1 minute, drain, rinse under cold water, and drain again.

4. In a large bowl, gently toss the potatoes, fiddleheads, red onion, chopped hard-cooked eggs, and dressing until well blended. Season with salt and freshly ground pepper to taste. Refrigerate the salad, covered, for 1 hour before serving.

SERVES 6 TO 8

SWEET CARROT SLAW

Shredded crisp carrots in a maple-flavored vinaigrette are a wonderful change from the traditional coleslaw. The Shakers would cook carrots and parsnips in syrup, and they often served any leftovers cold the next day, which inspired this recipe.

1 cup vegetable oil
⅓ cup maple syrup,
    preferably dark amber
    or grade B
⅓ cup white vinegar

2 teaspoons dried sweet
    basil or 1 tablespoon
    fresh opal basil
¼ cup diced onion

2 pounds carrots, peeled,
    shredded, and chilled
½ cups sliced scallions,
    including greens

2 tablespoons chopped
    fresh parsley
Salt and freshly ground
    pepper to taste

TO MAKE THE DRESSING

1. Combine the vegetable oil, maple syrup, vinegar, basil, and onion in a blender or food processor, and process until well blended, about 5 to 8 seconds. Refrigerate for at least 2 hours before using (see Note).

TO MAKE THE SLAW

2. In a large bowl, toss the shredded carrots, scallions, parsley, and vinaigrette until well blended. Season with salt and freshly ground pepper to taste. Serve chilled.

SERVES 6 TO 8

NOTE: The dressing may be made the day ahead; however, the salad is best served the day it is made.

CHILLED ASPARAGUS AND ORANGE SALAD WITH MINT VINAIGRETTE

This is a simple yet very refreshing salad. I prefer to feature it on our menu when native asparagus are in season.

Mint Vinaigrette (recipe
follows)
2 pounds thin asparagus,
trimmed

8 whole red leaf lettuce
leaves
2 cups orange segments

1. Fill a large saucepan half full with water and add a couple of pinches of salt. Heat to a boil over medium heat. Add the asparagus and cook for 2 to 3 minutes, or until tender. Drain and rinse with cold water. Drain again and refrigerate until needed. Refrigerate the orange segments until well chilled.

TO MAKE THE SALAD

2. In a large bowl, gently toss the asparagus, orange segments, and vinaigrette.

3. To serve the salad, line each plate with a lettuce leaf. Neatly arrange and evenly distribute the asparagus and orange segments. Evenly drizzle the excess vinaigrette over the salads. Serve chilled.

SERVES 6 TO 8

MINT VINAIGRETTE

⅔ cup vegetable oil
⅓ cup white vinegar
¼ cup honey

1 tablespoon sugar
½ cup fresh spearmint
leaves, washed

In a blender or food processor, combine the vegetable oil, vinegar, honey, sugar, and spearmint leaves, and blend for 5 to 8 seconds. Refrigerate the vinaigrette, covered, 1 hour, or until needed.

MAKES APPROXIMATELY 1¼ CUPS

CORN AND BLUEBERRY SALAD WITH CURRIED ORANGE VINAIGRETTE

Only one person could have created this unique concoction: James Haller, chef-founder of The Blue Strawbery Restaurant, in Portsmouth, New Hampshire, and our evening guest chef for the summer of 1988.

1 cup orange juice concentrate, thawed	2 cups fresh blueberries, washed, picked over, and chilled
2 tablespoons white vinegar	4 cups corn kernels (preferably fresh), chilled
¼ cup maple syrup, preferably dark amber or grade B	4 to 6 large Bibb lettuce leaves, washed and dried
Juice of ½ lime	
1 tablespoon curry powder	

1. In a blender or medium bowl, combine the orange juice concentrate, vinegar, maple syrup, lime juice, and curry powder, and blend for 5 to 8 seconds. Refrigerate, covered, for 1 hour, or until needed. The dressing can be made a day ahead and refrigerated until needed.

2. In a large bowl, combine the blueberries, corn, and dressing, and toss gently.

3. Place a lettuce leaf on each of the 4 to 6 serving dishes. Evenly distribute the corn and blueberry mixture onto the lettuce leaves. Serve immediately, chilled.

SERVES 4 TO 6

MIXED GREENS WITH ONION MAPLE BASIL VINAIGRETTE

Our house salad is a wonderful ever-changing mixture of lettuces, herbs, and flowers harvested fresh every morning from our own gardens. We toss it in our Shaker-inspired house dressing, a maple syrup–based sweet basil-flavored vinaigrette.

1½ cups vegetable oil
½ cup maple syrup, preferably dark amber or grade B
½ cup white vinegar
1 small onion, peeled and chopped

1 tablespoon dried sweet basil or 1½ tablespoons fresh opal basil

½ to ¾ pound mesclun, washed and dried (see Note)

TO MAKE THE VINAIGRETTE

1. In a blender or food processor, combine the vegetable oil, maple syrup, vinegar, chopped onion, and basil, and blend for 5 to 8 seconds. Refrigerate the vinaigrette, covered, at least 1 hour, or until needed.

TO MAKE THE SALAD

2. In a large bowl, gently toss the mesclun and ½ to 1 cup vinaigrette. Evenly distribute the mesclun on 8 serving plates.

SERVES 8

NOTE: Mesclun is a term used to describe a mixture of young greens and lettuces, fresh herbs, and flowers. The mixture often consists of ingredients like mustard greens, garden cress, arugula, pea tendrils, beet greens, baby kale, mâche, mint, apple blossoms, nasturtiums, New Zealand spinach, curly endive, chive blossoms, dill weed, dandelion greens, oak leaf lettuce, red romaine, Lolla Rossa, and on and on.

Mesclun is available in many produce sections of local supermarkets and at specialty stores. If premixed mesclun is unavailable, pick the freshest items from your local farmstand and create your own special mix.

SUGARING For over two hundred years the trees, sugar, or rock, maples, of the Shaker forest in Canterbury, New Hampshire, have given birth to the treasured sap responsible for the flavor, synonymous with New England, maple.

Some time between the end of February and the middle of March through mid-April, with cool nights and warm days, the ritual of "sugaring from the trees" begins. The maple harvest was one that all members of the Village would partake in ◇others would harness up the oxen and sleighs and head off into the Shaker forest (more than four thousand acres) to tap and hang handmade buckets on over eight hundred trees. The gathered sap was then boiled down in iron kettles back at the sugar camp by the Sisters, with the cleanup being left to the young girls, a joyous chore considering their fee, indulging in "fresh syrup on snow."

Despite the harvest season being a short one, the sweets of their labor were remembered throughout the year. From 1859–1860 Elder Henry Blinn decided to plant one maple tree for each new orphan girl who came to live with the Shakers. Her job was to hoe, water, and care for the tree year-round as it slowly grew. In May of 1864 Blinn also planted fifty maple trees out at Maple Grove. The Shakers always believed in leaving the earth a better place than they had found it. Thus planting new trees and caring for them would ensure many generations to come the pleasures they found from maple harvest season.

Although maple sugaring was a joyous occasion it was nonetheless a very vital one for the Shakers. Sugar, both white and brown, was often hard to come by and very expensive. Thus the Shakers relied on producing their own sweeteners. Many recipes had to be adapted using maple sugar, maple syrup, or honey as a substitute.

Today at The Creamery we still rely on locally produced maple syrup and honey as an integral part of our Shaker-inspired cooking.

FRIED GREEN TOMATO SALAD

The Shakers just dusted the tomato slices with seasoned flour, fried them in lard until golden brown, and served them with cream gravy. Incredibly, simply delicious.

Here the tomatoes are coated in a seasoned bread crumb mixture before they are panfried. They're great as a side dish, with cream gravy for a comforting lunch, or in this fall salad.

Herbal Vinaigrette, chilled (recipe follows)
2 cups fresh bread crumbs
1 cup grated Parmesan cheese
1 tablespoon chopped fresh parsley
Salt and freshly ground pepper to taste
4 large eggs
¼ cup milk
1 cup unbleached all-purpose flour
Vegetable oil for frying

3 green tomatoes, washed and each cut into 6 slices ¼ inch thick
8 to 9 cups mixed baby salad greens of choice
¼ cup thinly sliced white mushrooms
1 small red onion, peeled and thinly sliced
1 cup grated smoked Cheddar cheese
¼ cup slivered toasted almonds (optional)

1. Prepare the Herbal Vinaigrette.

TO MAKE THE FRIED TOMATOES

2. Combine the bread crumbs, Parmesan cheese, and parsley in a large bowl. Season with salt and freshly ground pepper to taste.

3. In a medium bowl, combine the eggs and milk, and mix until well blended. Put the flour in a shallow pan or bowl.

4. In a large frying pan, heat ¼ inch vegetable oil over medium heat. Dredge the tomato slices in the flour, dip them in the egg wash, and then coat them with the seasoned bread crumbs. Fry the tomato slices on both sides until light golden brown, approximately 45 to 60 seconds per side. Drain on paper towels and keep warm in a 200°F. oven.

TO MAKE THE SALAD

5. In a large bowl, combine the salad greens, mushrooms, and red onion. Toss the salad with the chilled vinaigrette. Divide the mixture evenly among 6 serving plates. Arrange 3 fried to-mato slices on each salad, and top with the grated cheese and toasted almonds, if desired. Serve immediately.

SERVES 6

HERBAL VINAIGRETTE

⅓ cup extra-virgin olive oil
2 tablespoons red wine
   vinegar
¼ teaspoon minced fresh
   garlic
1 teaspoon dried basil
1 teaspoon dried marjoram
1 teaspoon dried oregano
1 teaspoon sugar
⅛ teaspoon freshly ground
   pepper
¼ teaspoon salt

In a medium bowl or blender, combine all of the ingredients and mix until well blended, approximately 5 seconds. Refrigerate the vinaigrette, covered, at least 1 hour before serving, or until needed.

MAKES ABOUT ½ CUP

CURRIED SWEET POTATO SALAD

The inspiration for this creation comes from Sister Ethel's love of Waldorf salad. I substituted sweet potatoes for the apples, almonds for the walnuts, and added curry and coconut for that extra special touch. Needless to say, it was a winner with Sister Ethel.

2 pounds large sweet potatoes, scrubbed	**½ cup unsweetened coconut flakes**
½ cup sliced scallions, including greens	**¼ cup toasted slivered almonds**
½ cup raisins	**Salt and freshly ground pepper to taste**

CURRIED SOUR CREAM DRESSING

1 cup sour cream	**1 tablespoon honey**
1 tablespoon curry powder	**1 teaspoon chopped fresh parsley**
1 tablespoon white vinegar	
1 tablespoon sugar	

1. Bring a large pot of lightly salted water to a boil over medium heat. Add the sweet potatoes and cook for 30 minutes, or until tender when pierced with a knife. Drain and cool the potatoes, then peel them and cut into ¾-inch cubes.

TO MAKE THE DRESSING

2. In a medium bowl, combine the sour cream, curry powder, vinegar, sugar, honey, and parsley, and stir until smooth and well blended. Refrigerate, covered, until needed. The dressing can be made a day ahead and kept refrigerated.

TO MAKE THE SALAD

3. In a large bowl, combine the cubed sweet potatoes, scallions, raisins, coconut flakes, toasted almonds, and the dressing. Toss gently until well mixed. Season with salt and freshly ground pepper. Refrigerate, covered, until well chilled. The salad may be made a day ahead and kept refrigerated until needed.

SERVES 4 TO 6

HOME TOPICS

To Keep Lemons—Take good lemons, put them into an earthen vessel and pour on new butter-milk, covering well, set in a cool place, changing the butter-milk occasionally. We have found this a very excellent way for keeping them fresh.

THE SHAKER MANIFESTO   AUGUST 1882

CHILLED APPLE SLAW WITH CRANBERRY ORANGE PECAN DRESSING

The Shakers were always thinking up ways to use the many varieties of apples from their bountiful orchards. For this salad the apples are shredded like a traditional slaw. I think you'll find this slaw very intriguing.

One 14-ounce can whole cranberries in jelly
¼ cup orange juice concentrate, thawed

Juice of 1 lemon
1 cup pecan pieces
6 large Cortland or McIntosh apples, washed

1. In the bowl of a food processor, combine the cranberries in jelly, orange juice concentrate, lemon juice, and pecans, and process until just blended, approximately 5 seconds. Refrigerate the dressing, covered, 1 hour before using, or until needed. The dressing can be made a day ahead and refrigerated until needed.

2. Core and shred the apples in a food processor or with a hand grater. In a large bowl, combine the apples and dressing, and gently toss until thoroughly mixed. Serve immediately.

SERVES 6 TO 8

NOTE: This salad should be served the day it is made for best results.

CHILLED BAKED APPLES IN MINTED VINAIGRETTE

Originally created as a salad course, this dish also works extremely well with roast pork or baked country ham.

¾ cup maple syrup,
    preferably dark amber
    or grade B
¼ cup cider vinegar
  1 tablespoon minced fresh
    spearmint

4 large Cortland apples,
    washed
8 cups mixed baby salad
    greens of choice,
    washed and dried

TO BAKE THE APPLES

1. Preheat the oven to 400°F.

2. In a blender or small bowl, combine the maple syrup, vinegar, and spearmint, and blend for 5 to 8 seconds.

3. Core and halve the apples, and place in a baking dish, flat side down. Pour the dressing over the apples. Bake for 8 to 10 minutes, or until the apples start to soften but aren't overcooked. Remove the baking dish and allow to cool 15 minutes at room temperature. Place the baking dish in the refrigerator to chill 2 hours.

TO SERVE THE SALAD

4. Place 1 cup mixed baby salad greens on each of the 8 serving plates. Thinly slice each apple half, fan the slices across the salad greens, and drizzle the remaining dressing from the baking pan evenly over each salad. Serve chilled.

SERVES 8

NOTE: For best results this salad should be served the day it is made. To accompany hot entrées, do not chill the apples. Slice the apples while still hot and serve immediately over the greens.

STRAWBERRY AND CUCUMBER SALAD WITH HONEY LIME DRESSING

Customers ask over and over again, "What's in this salad?" They're always amazed when we answer, "Strawberries, cucumbers, honey, and limes." They don't understand how something with so few ingredients can taste so good. It's the Shaker way, pure and simple.

4 limes, sliced and seeded (rind on)
1 cup honey
3 medium cucumbers, washed

1 pint fresh strawberries, washed
6 large Bibb lettuce leaves, washed and dried

1. In a blender or food processor, combine the lime slices and honey, and blend for 5 to 8 seconds. Refrigerate, covered, 30 minutes.

2. Peel the cucumbers and cut in half lengthwise. Scoop out the seeds and slice the cucumbers into a bowl. Refrigerate, covered, 30 minutes.

3. Hull and quarter the strawberries. In a large bowl, combine the cucumbers, strawberries, and dressing, and toss gently.

4. Place a lettuce leaf on each of the 6 serving dishes. Evenly distribute the cucumber and strawberry mixture onto the lettuce leaves. Serve immediately.

SERVES 6

SLICED CUCUMBERS WITH MINTED LEMONADE DRESSING

This salad dressing was inspired by the Shakers' method of preparing lemonade. A lemon concentrate was made by simmering slices of lemon and fresh spearmint leaves in a simple syrup. This easy-to-transport concentrate was brought on picnics and out into the fields, and when combined with cold spring water, they had an instant thirst quencher.

In this salad a lemon concentrate is combined with cucumbers instead of cold spring water and is just as effective a relief on a hot summer day.

2 lemons, sliced and seeded (rind on)
1 cup white wine
3 cups sugar

¼ cup fresh spearmint leaves, washed
6 medium cucumbers
8 large Bibb lettuce leaves, washed and dried

1. In a large saucepan, combine the lemon slices, wine, and sugar over medium heat, and simmer until reduced by half, approximately 30 minutes. Carefully pour the hot mixture into a blender or food processor, add the spearmint leaves, and puree. Cool completely, then refrigerate, covered. The dressing can be made a day ahead and refrigerated until needed.

2. Peel the cucumbers and cut them in half lengthwise. Scoop out the seeds and slice the cucumbers into a large bowl. Refrigerate for 30 minutes, covered. Add the chilled lemon puree and toss with the cucumber slices until well blended.

3. Place a lettuce leaf on each of the 8 serving dishes. Evenly distribute the cucumber mixture onto the lettuce leaves. Serve chilled immediately.

SERVES 8

NOTE: This salad is best served directly after it is made.

CREAMY BUTTERMILK HERB DRESSING

The Canterbury Shakers first started selling garden seeds in 1829, and in their second herbal catalogue in 1847, they began offering dried culinary herbs, sweet marjoram, summer savory, sage, and thyme, packaged for retail sale.

The success of this salad dressing relies on the freshness of the herbs used. We cut them fresh daily in our herb gardens that have been flourishing for over two hundred years. This dressing is fantastic on any combination of mixed greens and for coleslaw, and will keep for up to three days in the refrigerator, covered.

1½ cups sour cream
1 cup mayonnaise
1¼ cups buttermilk
¼ cup white vinegar
2 tablespoons honey
1 tablespoon Dijon
   mustard
1 tablespoon finely
   chopped garlic

2 tablespoons chopped
   fresh parsley
2 tablespoons chopped
   fresh tarragon
2 tablespoons chopped
   fresh chives
2 tablespoons chopped
   fresh dill
Salt and freshly ground
   pepper to taste

In a large bowl, combine all of the ingredients and stir until well blended. Refrigerate the dressing, covered, for a minimum of 4 hours before serving.

MAKES APPROXIMATELY 4 CUPS

SLICED TOMATO SALAD WITH MINTED ORANGE DRESSING

I prefer to use Valencia or beefsteak tomatoes for this recipe, but you should feel free to try this recipe with whatever tomato is the freshest and most readily available to you.

1 cup orange juice concentrate, thawed	½ cup fresh spearmint leaves, washed
½ orange, sliced and seeded (rind on)	8 cups julienned spinach, washed
½ cup honey	4 large tomatoes, washed
Juice of ½ lemon	

TO MAKE THE DRESSING

1. In a blender or food processor, combine the orange juice concentrate, orange slices, honey, lemon juice, and spearmint leaves. Blend for 5 to 8 seconds and refrigerate, covered, for 1 hour.

TO SERVE THE SALAD

2. Place 1 cup julienned spinach on each of the 8 serving dishes. Core and thinly slice each tomato into 8 slices. Fan 4 slices of tomato over each plate of spinach. Drizzle the chilled dressing over the salads. Serve immediately.

SERVES 8

HOW TO MAKE TOMATO FIGS

Pour boiling water over the tomatoes in order to remove the skins; then weigh them and place them in a stone jar, with as much sugar as you have tomatoes, and let these stand two days; then pour off the syrup and boil and skim it until no skum rises. Then pour it over the tomatoes and let them stand for two days as before, then boil and skim again. After the third time, they are fit to dry, if the weather is good; if not let them stand in the syrup until drying weather. Then place on large earthen plates or dishes, and put them in the sun to dry, which will take about a week, after which pack them down in small wooden boxes, with fine white sugar between each layer. Tomatoes prepared in this manner will keep for years.

THE SHAKER MANIFESTO   DECEMBER 1882

FRESH DILL VINAIGRETTE

This basic vinaigrette goes well with mixed salad greens, chilled poached salmon, and shrimp. Try substituting fresh basil, mint, or tarragon for different tastes.

1 heaping tablespoon Dijon-style mustard	¾ cup vegetable oil
2 level tablespoons sugar	¼ cup white vinegar
2 tablespoons chopped fresh dill or 1 tablespoon dried	Pinch of salt

Combine all of the ingredients in a medium bowl. With a wire whisk beat the ingredients until they emulsify, about 20 seconds. Cover and refrigerate for at least 2 hours before using.

MAKES 1½ CUPS

COUNTRY-SMOKED BACON DRESSING

The key ingredient in this recipe is the high-quality bacon. I use either Vermont corncob-smoked or an oak-smoked bacon that's produced just a few miles north of the Village. Each type of bacon produces a distinctly different flavored dressing, but all are good. This is good on all kinds of lettuce salads.

1 pound smoked bacon, diced (see Sources)
1 medium onion, peeled and finely diced
1 teaspoon finely chopped garlic
1½ cups mayonnaise
1 cup light cream
1 tablespoon spicy brown mustard

2 tablespoons honey
4 tablespoons cider vinegar
2 tablespoons chopped fresh parsley
1 tablespoon minced scallions, greens only
Salt and freshly ground pepper to taste

1. In a large heavy frying pan, cook the bacon over medium heat. Just when the bacon starts to crisp, about 6 to 8 minutes, add the onion and garlic and continue to cook another 3 to 5 minutes. Drain off the fat and allow to cool about 15 minutes.

2. In a large bowl, combine the mayonnaise, cream, mustard, honey, vinegar, parsley, and scallions, and stir until well blended. Add the cooled bacon mixture and stir until well blended. Season to taste with salt and freshly ground pepper.

3. Refrigerate the dressing, covered, for a minimum of 4 hours before serving.

MAKES APPROXIMATELY 3½ CUPS

BREADS

Lily Belle of Canterbury

"BREAD WISDOM"

In baking bread, the most important point to consider is the yeast. Keep your yeast with care. Whenever possible, keep it in an icebox where it will be dry and cold. Though yeast may discolor at times, this in no way impairs its quality. So long as it is firm it is good to use. When it becomes too soft to handle, do not use it.

THE MIXING

Measure the liquid into a bowl and add the sugar. Sugar assists fermentation. Next, crumble yeast into the mixture. Allow to stand from six to eight minutes, add the shortening and sift enough flour to form a smooth light batter. Beat this thoroughly, so that the yeast may be well distributed. Salt may be dissolved or used dry.

THE KNEADING

The dough must not be chilled; therefore, knead quickly and lightly until it is smooth and elastic and does not stick to fingers or board.

THE RISING

After kneading, place dough in a bowl and set in a warm place, free from draught. Cover bowl to prevent crust from forming on dough, which could cause a streak in the bread. Let dough rise double in bulk.

THE MOLDING

Next, mold dough into loaves about half the size of pans. Put each loaf in a well-greased pan and let rise again in a warm place, free from draughts until double in size. To test if loaf is ready for oven, flour the finger and make an impression in loaf. If the impression disappears, give a little more time; if it remains, bread is ready to bake.

THE BAKING

Place in a quick oven where the loaf should brown in from fifteen to twenty minutes, then reduce the heat and bake more slowly. Bread is done when it leaves the sides of the pan. An ordinary-sized loaf should bake in one hour. Biscuits, rolls, etc., require a hotter oven than bread and should be baked fifteen or twenty minutes.

HELPFUL HINTS

Sponges should not be permitted to get too light. They are ready when bubbles gather on the surface and break occasionally.

After the loaf is baked, remove from the pan and let stand out of draught until cold.

To freshen stale bread, dip in cold water, then rebake in a quick oven.

(FROM ELDRESS BERTHA LINDSAY'S SCRAPBOOK)

CHEDDAR CHEESE AND CHIVE WAFERS

These cheese and herb wafers are best served straight from the oven with hot soup or a fresh garden salad. With a little imagination and experimentation, the flavor combinations are endless. Try Cheddar with sage, or pepper Jack with scallion for starters, and in the spirit of Shaker economy, use whatever is on hand.

8 ounces (about 2 cups) grated Vermont sharp Cheddar cheese
1 cup (2 sticks) unsalted butter, at room temperature
3 large egg yolks
1 teaspoon salt
1 to 2 tablespoons minced fresh chives
2 cups unbleached all-purpose flour

TO MAKE THE DOUGH

1. Combine the cheese, butter, egg yolks, salt, and chives in the bowl of a food processor. Process until the mixture becomes smooth. Then add the flour and process until the mixture forms a ball of dough.

2. Shape and roll the dough into a 2-inch-round cylinder. Wrap the dough in plastic wrap and refrigerate for 2 to 3 hours.

TO BAKE THE WAFERS

3. Preheat the oven to 400°F.

4. Slice the dough into ¼-inch-thick rounds. Place on an ungreased baking sheet and bake until lightly browned, about 5 to 8 minutes. Serve warm or at room temperature.

MAKES APPROXIMATELY 3 DOZEN WAFERS

Sour Cream Herb Biscuits

These biscuits are a variation on Sister Miriam Wall's favorite breakfast bread. Substituting sour cream for a portion of the butter gives these biscuits their light, moist, and airy texture. They are excellent as just plain table bread, or omit the herbs and use these biscuits as a base for a fresh berry shortcake.

2 cups pastry flour
1 tablespoon baking
powder
2 teaspoons sugar
1 teaspoon salt
⅔ cup grated Parmesan
cheese
1 tablespoon minced fresh
chives

1 tablespoon chopped
fresh parsley
2 tablespoons chilled
unsalted butter, cut in
½-inch cubes
1 cup sour cream
Melted butter for brushing
Kosher salt

1. Preheat the oven to 425°F.

2. Combine the flour, baking powder, sugar, salt, cheese, chives, parsley, and butter in the bowl of a food processor, and process to blend well. Add the butter to the flour mixture and pulse until it resembles a coarse meal. Add the sour cream and process until the mixture forms a ball of dough.

3. On a lightly floured surface, roll the dough out to a ¾- to 1-inch thickness. With a 2½-inch-round biscuit cutter, cut out biscuits. The excess dough can be rerolled once to cut more biscuits.

4. Place the biscuits on an ungreased baking sheet and bake 15 to 20 minutes, or until golden brown. Brush the tops of the warm biscuits with melted butter and sprinkle with kosher salt. Serve the biscuits warm.

MAKES 8 TO 10 BISCUITS

WHIPPED CREAM BISCUITS

Whipped cream biscuits were standard fare on the Canterbury Shakers' dining room tables. Most often the biscuits were served as breakfast starters with fresh butter and shaved maple sugar, or they accompanied chowders and stews at the evening meal.

These biscuits acquire their unique delicacy from substituting the traditional shortening (butter or lard) with lightly whipped heavy cream. Adding cream to biscuits is not a Shaker exclusive, but whipping the cream to lighten the texture is a Shaker innovation.

2 cups pastry flour
1 teaspoon salt

2 tablespoons baking
powder
1½ cups heavy cream

1. Preheat the oven to 400°F.

2. In a large bowl, sift together the flour, salt, and baking powder.

3. In another bowl, whip the heavy cream until soft peaks form. Gently fold the whipped cream into the dry ingredients with a fork.

4. Turn the dough out onto a lightly floured surface and knead the dough 3 to 5 times. Roll the dough out on a lightly floured surface to a ½- to ¾-inch thickness. Using a small, 2½-inch-round biscuit cutter, cut out as many biscuits as possible. Excess dough can be rerolled once to cut additional biscuits.

5. Place the biscuits on an ungreased baking sheet and bake for 15 to 20 minutes, or until golden brown. Serve the biscuits warm.

MAKES 12 BISCUITS

VARIATIONS

CHEESE WHIPPED CREAM BISCUITS
   Add ½ cup finely grated cheese, such as Parmesan or Cheddar, to the sifted flour mixture. Proceed as directed.

HERB WHIPPED CREAM BISCUITS
   Add 1 tablespoon minced fresh herbs of choice to the sifted flour mixture. Proceed as directed.

SHAKER RAISED SQUASH BISCUITS

This was Eldress Bertha's favorite bread. We feature it daily at the restaurant and sell out of it every day at the bakery.

1 cup milk
4 tablespoons (½ stick) unsalted butter
¾ cup sugar
½ teaspoon salt
1 yeast cake or 1 envelope dry yeast
4 to 5 cups unbleached all-purpose flour

1½ cups fresh butternut squash or pumpkin puree, strained, or one 16-ounce can pureed pumpkin or squash
2 large eggs, at room temperature
Melted butter for brushing

1. In a heavy saucepan, heat the milk and butter over medium heat until the butter is melted. Remove from the heat.

2. In a large bowl, mix the sugar and salt, and pour the hot milk mixture over. Stir and allow to cool, uncovered, to luke-warm. Add the yeast and 2 cups flour. Beat with a mixer at medium speed for 2 minutes, or stir to blend well. Add the squash and eggs, mixing well. Continue to add flour until you have a stiff dough that begins to leave the sides of the bowl.

3. Turn the dough out onto a lightly floured surface and knead by hand for 7 to 8 minutes, using additional flour as needed to prevent sticking. Put the dough into a lightly greased bowl. Turn the dough so that all sides are greased and cover with a towel. Let the dough rise in a warm place until doubled in volume, about 1½ hours. Punch down the dough, and roll out on a lightly floured surface to a ½-inch thickness. With a floured 2½-inch biscuit cutter, cut out as many biscuits as possible.

4. Place the biscuits in a lightly greased 8- by 8-inch pan with the sides touching for soft sides or on a lightly greased baking sheet a few inches apart from each other for browned sides. Cover with a towel and let rise until doubled again, about 1 hour. Meanwhile, preheat the oven to 425°F. Bake 25 minutes, or until golden brown. Brush the tops of the biscuits with the melted butter while hot, and serve immediately or cool on a wire rack.

MAKES 2½ TO 3 DOZEN BISCUITS

SISTER EUNICE CLARK'S EXCELLENT DOUGHNUTS

Although Sister Eunice often helped with the cooking and selling of baked beans and brown bread, cooking was never one of her favorite chores. You would never know it by the doughnuts she made!

1 cup milk	½ teaspoon salt
1 cup sugar	½ teaspoon grated nutmeg
2 large eggs, beaten	1 teaspoon ground
1 teaspoon butter,	cinnamon
softened	2 quarts vegetable oil for
3½ cups unbleached	frying
all-purpose flour	1 cup sugar mixed with
2 teaspoons baking powder	1 teaspoon ground
1 teaspoon baking soda	cinnamon (optional)

1. In a large bowl, stir together the milk, sugar, eggs, and butter.

2. In another large bowl, sift together the flour, baking powder, baking soda, salt, nutmeg, and cinnamon. Gradually add to the milk mixture, beating well to form a stiff dough.

3. Roll the dough out on a lightly floured board to a ½- to ⅝-inch thickness. With a floured 3-inch doughnut cutter, cut out as many doughnuts as possible. Reserve the doughnut holes. The dough may be rerolled to cut additional doughnuts.

4. Preheat the oil in a fryer to 375°F., or heat at least 2 inches of oil in a deep skillet to 375°F., making sure the oil reaches no more than halfway up the sides of the skillet. Lower the doughnuts into the hot oil with a spatula, cooking 2 or 3 doughnuts at a time. Cook for 1½ minutes, until golden brown on the underside, then turn once and cook for 1½ minutes more.

5. Drain on paper towels. Warm doughnuts may be shaken in a bag with the cinnamon-sugar mixture, if desired.

MAKES ABOUT 1½ DOZEN DOUGHNUTS

L E M O N – P O P P Y S E E D –
S O U R C R E A M M U F F I N S

Sister Ethel Hudson loved any and all baked goods that were made with sour cream so I created these muffins especially for her. Like most muffins, these are best served warm.

¾ teaspoon salt
1 cup sugar, plus extra for sprinkling
2 large eggs
1 cup sour cream
3 tablespoons vegetable oil
1 tablespoon lemon extract

1 teaspoon vanilla extract
1 tablespoon lemon zest
¼ cup poppy seeds
1½ cups unbleached all-purpose flour
½ teaspoon baking powder
⅓ teaspoon baking soda

1. Preheat the oven to 400°F. Grease 12 muffin tins or line with paper liners.

2. In a large bowl, combine the salt, sugar, and eggs, and whisk until foamy. Stir in the sour cream, oil, lemon and vanilla extracts, lemon zest, and poppy seeds.

3. Sift the flour, baking powder, and baking soda into a bowl, and gently stir into the sour cream mixture, taking care not to overmix the batter.

4. Fill the muffin tins three-quarters full with batter. Sprinkle the tops of the muffins with additional sugar and bake the muffins 20 to 25 minutes, or until lightly browned. Serve warm.

MAKES 12 MUFFINS

WILD BLUEBERRY MUFFINS

During the peak harvest of wild blueberries, July and August, we make these muffins seven days a week and wait for them to bake with unwaveringly high anticipation. Everyone has their favorite recipe and this book wouldn't be complete without including ours.

2 cups unbleached all-purpose flour	**¼ cup vegetable oil**
1 cup sugar, plus extra for sprinkling	**1 large egg, lightly beaten**
1 tablespoon baking powder	**1 cup milk**
½ teaspoon salt	**2 cups fresh wild blueberries, washed and picked over**

1. Preheat the oven to 400°F. Grease 12 large muffin tins or line with paper liners.

2. In a large bowl, sift together the flour, sugar, baking powder, and salt. Gently stir in the oil, egg, and milk, taking care not to overmix the batter. Gently fold in the blueberries.

3. Fill the muffin tins three-quarters full with batter. Sprinkle the tops of the muffins with extra sugar and bake 20 to 25 minutes, or until lightly browned. Serve warm.

MAKES 12 LARGE MUFFINS

SHAKER SAGE CAKES

These little cakes, created by Sister Frances Hall of Hancock Shaker Village, are actually more like fritters. I love them best served as a side dish to Applewood Smoked Loin of Pork with Spicy Fried Apples or Chunky Applesauce (page 54) or with fried eggs and sausage for breakfast.

4 tablespoons unbleached all-purpose flour	**1 large egg, separated**
¼ teaspoon salt	**1 tablespoon chopped fresh sage leaves**
1 tablespoon sugar	**Vegetable oil for frying**
6 tablespoons water	

1. Sift the flour, salt, and sugar into a medium bowl. Add the water and egg yolk, and mix to a smooth paste. Mix in the chopped sage leaves, cover, and set aside to rest for 30 minutes.

2. When ready to serve, in a small bowl beat the egg white until stiff but not dry and fold into the batter until well mixed.

3. Heat 2 inches of oil in a deep skillet to 375°F. over medium heat. Drop the batter by teaspoons into the hot oil, cooking 3 to 4 cakes at a time. Fry the cakes until golden brown on both sides, about 1 minute per side. Drain the cakes on paper towels and serve immediately.

MAKES APPROXIMATELY 12 CAKES

BANANA NUT BREAD

This bread is great for breakfast, snacking, and an irresistible indulgence griddled and served with Warm Banana Pecan Compote over Vanilla Bean Ice Cream (page 153).

½ cup (1 stick) unsalted
   butter, softened
½ cup light brown sugar
½ cup granulated sugar
2 large eggs
1 cup mashed banana
   puree
1 teaspoon vanilla extract

2 cups unbleached
   all-purpose flour
1 tablespoon baking
   powder
½ teaspoon salt
1 cup pecan or walnut
   pieces

1. Preheat the oven to 350°F. Lightly grease a large loaf pan.

2. In a large bowl, cream the butter and sugars until smooth. Add the eggs, mashed bananas, and vanilla extract, and mix well.

3. In another large bowl, sift together the flour, baking powder, and salt, and add this mixture to the creamed mixture. Mix just until the batter is combined. Gently fold in the nuts.

4. Pour the batter into the lightly greased baking pan and bake for 45 to 50 minutes, or until the top of the bread springs back up when pressed with a finger.

MAKES 1 LOAF

GRIST MILL Indians had been pounding corn into samp for over two hundred years before the Pilgrims first set up housekeeping in Plymouth, Massachusetts, in 1620. For years the Pilgrims used the Indians' time-tested method of pounding corn. It wasn't until about fifty years later, when the Pilgrims were confident of their dominant status and potential for continental expansion, that small mills began to spring up where there was a reliable source of

water power. Once a mill became established, villages often sprung up around them.

As America changed in the nineteenth century, American milling changed as well. Village mills designed to fill the needs of villagers and local farmers gave way to merchant mills, mills geared for volume and profit. Many village mills closed up as competition from larger mills rendered them obsolete. By 1900 many water-powered mills were more curiosities than viable businesses, more valuable as historical sites than for any flour or feed they might still produce.

Gray's Grist Mill in Adamsville, Rhode Island, survives as a direct link to the village mills of the early 1800s. Primitive in many ways, it has changed little over the centuries. The milling room still has two sets of stones, one for flours and one for feed, although the feed stones no longer turn. Once the peripheral business of the mill, Gray's Mill now produces only stone-ground flours exclusively for the country's top chefs and devoted retail customers.

Since 1982 Tim McTague has been the miller and spirit behind this small mill. With the support of owner Ralph Guild, Gray's Grist Mill continues in the tradition that began on that site in 1675. However, instead of water power Tim has ingeniously devised a way to hook up a 1946 Dodge truck motor to power the mill, with a stick wedged against the accelerator to keep the engine running. The Shakers would be proud!

In 1795 the Canterbury Shakers erected a grist mill for grinding flours and feed, not only for their uses but for sale as well. Today all that remains is the granite foundation and the memories shared with us by the Sisters. The Sisters often spoke of their dissatisfaction with the machine-milled flours of today, and how they lacked the taste and texture of flours from days long since past. When I first came to the village one of my priorities was to seek out purveyors capable of supplying the quality ingredients necessary to maintain the Shaker's high standards of excellence. Gray's Grist Mill received the Shakers' seal of approval for their stone-ground flours.

OLD-FASHIONED STEAMED BROWN BREAD

Today our brown bread is as close as possible to that of the Canterbury Shakers, thanks to miller Tim McTague of Gray's Grist Mill in Adamsville, Rhode Island. Tim provides our bake-shop with the freshly stone-ground cornmeal, rye, and whole wheat flour necessary to make authentic brown bread. In place of Tim's excellent Brown Bread Flour Mix you may create a blend of the appropriate flours.

Try this New England classic the next time you put a pot of baked beans on. The preparation is simple and the results peerless. Leftovers are delicious toasted and buttered as part of a hearty New England breakfast.

2 cups Gray's Brown Bread Flour Mix (see Note and Sources)
2 teaspoons baking soda
Pinch of salt

1 tablespoon sugar
1½ cups milk
½ cup molasses
½ cup chopped raisins

1. In a large pot with a lid, bring 2 inches of water to a simmer over medium-low heat. Generously grease a 1-pound coffee can.

2. In a large bowl, combine the flour mix, baking soda, salt, and sugar.

3. In another bowl, mix the milk and molasses together. Pour over the dry ingredients, mixing gently to form a smooth batter. Gently fold in the raisins. Pour the batter into the greased coffee can and cover the can tightly with aluminum foil. Place the can in the pot of simmering water, cover the pot, and steam for 2½ to 3 hours, or until the loaf is firm to the touch. Cool the bread 1 to 1½ hours before unmolding, then unmold and cool the bread completely on a wire rack before serving.

MAKES 1 LOAF

NOTE: Gray's Brown Bread Flour Mix can be substituted with equal parts of ground cornmeal, rye meal, and whole wheat flour to make up the 2 cups.

HONEY–WHOLE WHEAT BREAD

Freshly baked bread is my downfall. Within minutes of removing it from the oven I'm smothering steaming slices with butter.

This recipe relies on the quality of the stone-ground whole wheat flour we use from Gray's Grist Mill (see Sources).

2¼ cups milk	1 tablespoon salt
1 tablespoon molasses	3 cups unbleached bread
2 tablespoons honey	flour
1 tablespoon dry yeast	3 cups stone-ground whole
¼ cup vegetable oil	wheat flour

1. In a large heavy saucepan, scald the milk over medium-high heat. Cool the milk to lukewarm, then add the molasses, honey, and yeast. Stir in the oil and salt and add the flour 1 cup at a time, mixing well after each addition.

2. Knead the dough on a lightly floured surface until the dough becomes smooth and elastic, about 7 to 8 minutes. Place the dough in a lightly oiled bowl, turning to cover the dough with oil completely. Cover with a towel and allow the dough to rise in a warm place until doubled, about 1½ hours.

3. Punch down the dough and shape it into 2 loaves. Place the loaves into two lightly greased large baking pans, cover with a towel, and allow to rise until doubled in size, about 1 hour. Meanwhile, preheat the oven to 350°F.

4. Bake the bread 45 to 60 minutes. To test for doneness, tap the bottom of the loaf; if it sounds hollow, the bread is done.

MAKES 2 LOAVES

JONNY CAKES

Gray's Grist Mill has been turning out Rhode Island Jonny Cake Meal since 1878. Natives of the state, as well as anyone who still longs for the taste of real jonny cakes, are glad to know that some of the fields of Little Compton, Rhode Island, still yield golden harvests of Narragansett Indian Flint Corn, and that a little mill by a pond in nearby Adamsville still grinds true Rhode Island Jonny Cake Meal.

We offer jonny cakes on our Sunday brunch menu accompanied by local maple syrup, fried eggs, and rashers of locally smoked bacon. They are unrivaled as our biggest seller every Sunday.

Jonny cakes should be crunchy on both sides and creamy with a rich corn flavor inside. The recipe that follows is from Tim the miller. Who would better know how to make these treats?

1 cup jonny cake meal or white cornmeal (see Sources)	¾ cup boiling water
	¼ cup milk
	1 tablespoon heavy cream
¼ teaspoon salt	2 tablespoons vegetable oil

1. In a medium bowl, combine the jonny cake meal or white cornmeal and salt and stir in the boiling water. Let rest for a few minutes, uncovered. Add the milk and cream, and stir until well blended.

2. Heat a cast-iron griddle over medium-high heat, or heat an electric griddle to 375°F. Pour the oil onto the cooking surface of the griddle and tilt to evenly disperse the oil.

3. Drop the batter by spoonfuls onto the griddle to form 3½- to 4-inch-round cakes, and then resist the urge to flip them or move them around for about 4 to 5 minutes. Jonny cakes have a tendency to stick sometimes and leaving them alone helps alleviate this problem. Flip them over to cook on the other side for about 4 minutes more. Serve them warm with everything from maple syrup to poached eggs and caviar.

MAKES 10 TO 12 FOUR-INCH CAKES

KITCHEN EDUCATION

The origin of many of the troubles which afflict man-kind may be traced to a disordered stomach. No doubt but some of our bad legislation may be attributed to indigestible hotel breakfasts, and the burdens of sorrow produced by social disturbances have no more prolific contributor than the disordered stomach which pro-duces disordered minds. To raise the average of mortal-ity, happiness and prosperity of the people, the science of eating *must be given a more prominent place in our educational system. Through ignorance, and much of it inexcusable, we eat disease, we drink it, and breathe it. What to eat, how to cook it and when and how to eat it, are certainly subjects of study, quite as practical and beneficial as the conjugation of Greek verbs.*

Isn't it a little strange that while we employ the best medical skill we can obtain to cure disease, we turn our stomachs over to ignorant cooks and allow them to cram it with dietetic abominations which ruin its functions and produce disease?

*If talent, genius and skill are looking for a good mis-sionary field, the kitchen is the great uncivilized realm. We want the coming generation of girls taught how to cook intelligently. Give the stomach good, wholesome food, and it will fill your veins with pure blood, which in turn will give you a healthy brain and drive away the whole brood of manufactured troubles. We have had education for the parlor, and we are a nation of dyspeptics. Now, as a matter of experiment let us try education for the kitchen—*Western Plowman.

THE SHAKER MANIFESTO   SEPTEMBER 1883

Sweet Fennel Corn Bread

Corn bread in its many forms and varieties has always been very popular with the Shakers.

This is a fun bread to make because it's baked in a cast-iron skillet, producing a buttery bottom crust and a golden brown top crust. While this is an easy recipe, you must work fast. The batter must be mixed together quickly and turned into the frying pan while it's still hot.

1¼ cups jonny cake meal or white cornmeal (see Sources)
1 cup unbleached all-purpose flour
½ teaspoon salt
4 teaspoons baking powder

2 tablespoons lightly toasted fennel seeds
2 large eggs, beaten
1 cup milk
3 tablespoons honey
5 tablespoons unsalted butter

1. Preheat the oven to 400°F.

2. In a medium bowl, combine the jonny cake meal or white cornmeal, flour, salt, baking powder, and fennel seeds. In a large bowl, mix the eggs, milk, and honey.

3. Put the butter in a 10-inch cast-iron frying pan and place the pan in the oven until the butter is melted, watching that it doesn't burn. Remove the hot frying pan from the oven and tilt it so the hot butter covers the sides of the pan.

4. Add the dry ingredients to the milk mixture and pour in the hot butter from the pan, mixing together quickly. Pour the batter into the hot frying pan and bake 25 to 30 minutes, or until golden brown. Serve warm or at room temperature.

MAKES ONE 10-INCH BREAD

MEATS

APPLEWOOD SMOKED LOIN OF PORK WITH *SPICY FRIED* APPLES OR *C*HUNKY APPLESAUCE

This dish is a longtime standard on our fall menu at The Cream-ery. The recipe involves two days of preparation, but it's well worth the extra effort.

Apples are a favorite fruit of the Shakers, appearing in savory and sweet dishes with regularity. The Shakers loved roast pork or ham with apples, but I smoke the pork loin in this adaptation.

This recipe was tested using the Little Chief home smoker (see Sources).

BRINE II

2 quarts water
½ cup kosher salt
1¼ cups sugar
3 bay leaves
1 tablespoon finely
   chopped garlic

2 tablespoons minced fresh
   shallots
1 tablespoon whole
   allspice berries
1 tablespoon hot pepper
   sauce

3-pound boneless center-
   cut pork loin roast

Spicy Fried Apples (page
   166) or Chunky
   Applesauce (page 165)

TO MAKE THE BRINE

1. In a large saucepan combine the water, kosher salt, sugar, bay leaves, garlic, shallots, allspice, and hot pepper sauce and bring to a boil over high heat. Turn off the heat and cool completely. Submerge the pork loin in the brine, cover the saucepan, and refrigerate for a minimum of 16 hours and a maximum of 24 hours.

2. Remove the pork loin from the brine, rinse under cold water, and pat dry. The loin may be refrigerated, well wrapped, until ready to smoke, up to 1 day.

TO SMOKE THE PORK LOIN

3. Place the brined pork loin on the top shelf of the smoker. Follow the instructions included with the smoker and begin smoking the pork loin using the first of 3 pans of applewood chunks total. Rotate pans as directed.

4. When the smoking process is complete, immediately remove the smoked pork loin from the smoker. The pork loin is *NOT* cooked during the smoking process and therefore must be roasted in the oven or wrapped in foil and refrigerated. (The pork loin should be cooked the same day it is smoked.)

TO ROAST THE PORK LOIN

5. Preheat the oven to 375°F.

6. Put the smoked pork loin in a roasting pan and roast for 45 minutes, or until the meat has an internal temperature of 155°F. on a meat thermometer. Remove the pork loin from the oven, cover loosely with aluminum foil, and allow to rest for 7 to 10 minutes before slicing. Serve thinly sliced pork with Spicy Fried Apples on the side or with Chunky Applesauce.

SERVES 6 TO 8

GRILLED PORK CHOPS WITH CRANBERRY MAPLE SAUCE

Maple syrup nicely offsets the very tart flavor of native cranberries. With fresh berries available October through December, this dish gives us the perfect excuse to fire up the old barbecue grill one more time before it is completely retired for warmer days.

BRINE I

2 quarts water
½ cup kosher salt
1¼ cups sugar
3 bay leaves
1 tablespoon finely
  chopped garlic

2 tablespoons minced
  shallots
1 tablespoon whole
  allspice berries
2 teaspoons hot pepper
  sauce

8 center-cut pork chops
  (2 inches thick each)

Cranberry Maple Sauce
  (recipe follows)

TO MAKE THE BRINE

1. Combine all of the ingredients in a large saucepan and bring to a boil over high heat. Turn off the heat and cool the brine completely in a stainless steel or plastic container. Submerge the pork chops in the brine and cover. Refrigerate for a minimum of 16 hours and a maximum of 24 hours.

2. Remove the pork chops from the brine, rinse under cold water, and pat dry.

3. Grill the chops over medium heat (see To Grill the Chicken, page 76) to your liking, about 5 to 6 minutes per side for medium doneness. Serve the pork chops hot with Cranberry Maple Sauce.

SERVES 8

CRANBERRY MAPLE SAUCE

One 12-ounce bag
  cranberries, washed and
  picked over

1¼ cups maple syrup,
  preferably dark amber
  or grade B
1 tablespoon Dijon
  mustard

1. Combine the berries and maple syrup in a large heavy saucepan. Bring to a boil over medium-high heat and cook until the berries burst, about 5 to 7 minutes.

2. Remove from the heat and stir in the mustard. Serve hot or at room temperature.

MAKES APPROXIMATELY 2 CUPS

BAKED COUNTRY-SMOKED HAM WITH SPICED CHERRY CATSUP

Baked hams have always appeared on Shaker dinner tables during the holiday season, since the Shakers used to raise, cure, and smoke their own hams. What I like about country-smoked hams is the lack of preparation involved. They require no soaking in water like their southern counterparts, just simple baking.

By far, my favorite accompaniment for ham is Spiced Cherry Catsup. The catsup can either be poured over the ham during the last thirty minutes of cooking to form a caramelized glaze, or served on the side of the sliced ham.

One 8- to 10-pound country smoked ham (see Sources)

Spiced Cherry Catsup (recipe follows)

Preheat the oven to 325°F. Place the ham in a large roasting pan. Bake the ham in the oven for 20 minutes per pound (about 3 hours for a 9-pound ham). Carve the ham and serve warm or at room temperature with Spiced Cherry Catsup.

SERVES 8 WITH PLENTY OF LEFTOVERS

SPICED CHERRY CATSUP

10 whole allspice berries
8 whole cloves
Two 4-inch cinnamon sticks
1½ quarts fresh Bing cherries, washed and pitted

2 cups granulated sugar
2 cups maple or light brown sugar
1 cup white vinegar
1 tablespoon almond extract

1. Tie the allspice, cloves, and cinnamon in a piece of cheesecloth.

2. Roughly chop the cherries by hand or in a food processor.

3. In a large heavy saucepan, combine the spice bag, sugars, and vinegar, and bring to a boil over medium-high heat, stirring frequently. Add the cherries and simmer over medium-low heat

until the mixture starts to thicken, 50 to 60 minutes, stirring often.

4. Remove the spice bag and stir in the almond extract. Can the Spiced Cherry Catsup using the boiling-water method (following).

MAKES 4 TO 5 HALF PINTS

BOILING-WATER BATH CANNING METHOD

This method of processing canned items is basically for fruits. You'll need a water-bath canner, a special pot with a lid and a wire rack insert that holds the canning jars. I prefer to use jars with two-piece vacuum lids because it's easy to tell if they've sealed properly as the center of the caps sink down. If you press the center of the lid and it moves up and down, the jar has not been sealed properly.

TO CAN THE CATSUP

1. As the catsup is cooking, sterilize five ½-pint jars and lids. They should be thoroughly washed and then simmered in 180°F. water. The jars and two-piece vacuum lids should stay in the hot water until the catsup is ready to be jarred.

2. Pour the hot catsup into the hot jars leaving ¼ inch of headspace. Use a knife to stir to remove any air bubbles that might be trapped in the jars. Place the two-piece vacuum lids on the jars following the manufacturer's instructions. Place the jars into the canner filled with hot water. The water must cover the jars by a minimum of one inch. Place the lid on the canner, heat to a boil, and cook for 10 minutes.

3. When the 10-minute processing time is complete, remove the jars from the canner. Allow the jars to cool completely, then check to see if the sealing process is complete. Allow the catsup to age one week before serving. If the seal ruptures or the top of the jar pops up at any time, discard the jar immediately.

POT ROAST OF BEEF WITH ONION-SAGE GRAVY

For one reason or another this dish has fallen by the wayside. Pot roast really deserves a lot more credit than it receives. It utilizes an inexpensive cut of meat, the preparation is minimal, and the results are exquisite—a very Shaker dish as it yields maximum flavor and appeal with relatively small effort.

Actually, the best thing about cooking a pot roast of beef is serving the leftovers the next day for lunch. Slices of pot roast make great hot or cold sandwiches.

4 tablespoons vegetable oil	**2 tablespoons minced fresh**
One 4½-pound bottom	**sage**
round or chuck beef	**1 cup red wine**
roast	**1 quart beef stock**
2 medium onions, peeled	**Salt and freshly ground**
and diced	**pepper to taste**
4 tablespoons unbleached	
all-purpose flour	

1. Preheat the oven to 325°F.

2. Heat the oil in a braising pan or large roasting pan with a lid over high heat. Sear the meat in the hot oil, turning so all sides are browned, then set the meat aside.

3. Lower the heat to medium, add the onions, and cook until browned, about 5 to 7 minutes. Stir in the flour and cook for 2 to 3 minutes, stirring often. Add the sage, wine, and stock, and stir until smooth.

4. Return the meat to the pan and heat to a boil over medium heat. Cover the pan and place in the oven to braise until fork-tender, about 2½ to 3 hours. Turn the meat a couple of times during the cooking process.

5. Remove the cooked meat to a platter, skim the fat off the top of the liquid in the pan, and reduce the sauce by approximately half over medium heat to make a rich gravy. Season with salt and pepper. Slice the beef against the grain ¼ inch thick and serve with the pan gravy.

SERVES 6 TO 8

POT ROAST OF BEEF WITH GINGERSNAP GRAVY

Pot roast of beef was a favorite of the Shaker Brothers and hired men alike. Eldress Bertha made pot roast often and inspired me to rediscover this great dish and method of cooking. In this variation the unusual addition of gingersnap cookies are used to flavor and thicken the natural pan juices.

4 tablespoons vegetable oil
One 4½-pound bottom
    round or chuck beef
    roast
2 medium onions, peeled
    and diced
1 teaspoon chopped garlic
4 tablespoons unbleached
    all-purpose flour
4 cups beef stock

½ cup finely diced carrots
¼ cup finely diced celery
2 tablespoons light brown
    sugar
8 to 10 two-inch
    gingersnap cookies,
    crushed
Salt and freshly ground
    pepper to taste

1. Preheat the oven to 325°F.

2. Heat the oil in a braising pan or large roasting pan with a lid over medium-high heat. Sear the meat in the hot oil, turning so all sides are browned, then set the meat aside.

3. Add the onions and garlic, and cook until browned, about 5 to 7 minutes. Stir in the flour and cook 2 to 3 minutes, stirring often. Add the stock and stir until smooth. Add the carrots, celery, brown sugar, and crushed cookies, and heat to a simmer over medium heat, stirring often. Add the meat, cover, and braise in the oven 2½ to 3 hours, or until fork-tender. Turn the meat a couple of times during the cooking process.

4. Remove the cooked meat to a platter, skim the grease off the top of the gravy, and reduce, if necessary. Season with salt and pepper. Slice the beef against the grain ¼ inch thick and serve with the pan gravy.

SERVES 6 TO 8

TARRAGON SWISS STEAKS

Braising has become a less common method of cooking these days, but the Shakers used this technique frequently, knowing it was a great way to turn inexpensive cuts of meat, like cube steaks, into tender, flavorful steaks with simple preparation and little attention during cooking. This cooking method is worth rediscovering. Try these served over buttered noodles or with seasoned mashed potatoes.

3 tablespoons vegetable oil	2 cups beef stock
4 cube steaks (8 ounces each)	1 tablespoon tomato paste
1 large onion, peeled and diced	1 tablespoon Dijon mustard
3 tablespoons unbleached all-purpose flour	1 tablespoon chopped fresh tarragon
1 cup red wine	Salt and freshly ground pepper to taste

1. Preheat the oven to 350°F.

2. Heat the oil in a braising pan or large roasting pan with a lid over medium heat. Sear the steaks for 1 minute on each side and set the meat aside.

3. Add the onion to the pan and cook until browned, about 5 to 7 minutes. Stir in the flour and cook 2 to 3 minutes, stirring often. Add the wine, stock, tomato paste, mustard, and tarragon, and stir until smooth. Heat to a simmer over medium heat and add the steaks. Cover the pan and braise the steaks in the oven for 1½ hours, or until the steaks are fork-tender.

4. Remove the steaks from the pan. Skim the grease from the top of the sauce, reduce the sauce, if necessary, and season with salt and pepper. Serve the steaks with the sauce.

SERVES 4

NORTHWOOD VEAL STEW

With all the controversy over veal these days, I don't often include it on the menu. But when I do, I always get my veal from Margie's Naturally Raised Veal (see Sources). The calves range freely with Jersey nurse cows and are 100 percent free of hormones, antibiotics, or pesticides of any kind.

This is a good old-fashioned, hearty stew that can be made with either root or spring vegetables, depending on the season. Serve the stew over hot buttered noodles, Herbed Rice Pilaf (page 124), or simply in a large bowl with hot biscuits on the side.

3 tablespoons vegetable oil
2 pounds naturally raised
   veal stew meat, cut into
   1- to 1½-inch cubes
2 medium onions, peeled
   and diced
3 tablespoons unbleached
   all-purpose flour
3 cups beef stock
1 tablespoon tomato paste
1 tablespoon chopped
   fresh tarragon

1 tablespoon chopped
   fresh parsley
3 cups ½-inch diced or
   sliced vegetables, such
   as potatoes, carrots,
   turnips, peas, or
   mushrooms
1 cup sour cream
Salt and freshly ground
   pepper to taste

1. Preheat the oven to 350°F.

2. Heat the oil in a braising pan or roasting pan with a lid over high heat. Sear the meat in the hot oil, turning so the meat browns on all sides, then set the meat aside.

3. Add the onions and brown over medium-high heat, about 5 to 7 minutes. Stir in the flour and cook for 2 to 3 minutes, stirring often. Add the stock, tomato paste, tarragon, and parsley, and stir until smooth. Bring to a simmer over medium heat, add the meat, cover, and braise in the oven for 1 hour.

4. Remove the pan from the oven, add the vegetables, then return the pan to the oven, covered. Braise for another 1 to 1½ hours, or until the meat is tender. Stir in the sour cream, season with salt and pepper, and serve hot.

SERVES 4

MEALTIME During the twentieth century the main kitchen was staffed with a First cook who planned the menus and prepared the main dishes, a Second cook who assisted and prepared side dishes, a Messer who cooked for the sick and elderly with meal restrictions, two cooks in the bakery room, one making breads and the other making desserts, and a couple of young girls as servers.

The main dining room originally had five long trestle tables, each seating twelve, extending the length of the room. An additional table for twelve was set off in the corner near the wood stove for the elderly members. Meals were served family-style and you were allowed to eat as much as you liked as long as you "Shaker[ed] your plate," taking only what you could eat and leaving nothing to waste.

Meals were served in seatings. At approximately a quarter before the noon hour the dinner bell was rung to summon the men in from the fields and workshops. They would quickly clean up and go to the Brethren Retiring room to say the noon prayer and await the second bell summoning them to the dining room. The Sisters and children would wait in the Sisters Retiring room and go through the same rituals as the Brothers before being served at the second seating. The cooking staff generally ate in the kitchen.

SPICY LAMB MEATBALLS

Here's a fairly inexpensive way to savor the great taste of lamb. These meatballs simmered in Fresh Tomato Sauce (page 163) can be served over fresh pasta for dinner or as a sandwich for a simple, hearty lunch.

1½ pounds fresh ground
    lamb
1 cup fresh bread crumbs
2 large eggs, beaten
¼ cup minced onion
1 tablespoon minced garlic
½ teaspoon chili powder
½ teaspoon ground cumin

½ teaspoon crumbled dried
    rosemary
1 tablespoon chopped
    fresh parsley
¼ teaspoon ground
    cayenne pepper
    (optional)
1½ teaspoons salt

1. Preheat the oven to 350°F.

2. In a large bowl, combine all of the ingredients and mix well. Shape the mixture into 12 two-inch balls.

3. Place the meatballs in a baking pan and bake for 20 minutes, or until cooked through. Remove the meatballs from the baking dish and drain on paper towels. Serve hot.

MAKES 12 TWO-INCH MEATBALLS

VARIATION

To serve with tomato sauce, simmer the cooked meatballs in 1 pint of your favorite tomato sauce. Allow 3 meatballs and ½ cup sauce per serving, and serve over hot pasta or in a large sandwich roll with grated Parmesan cheese.

THE SHAKERS' FINE COOKERY
BY SISTER MARCIA

In order to understand the excellence of Shaker food one must know something of the intelligence and the system employed in its preparation. The kitchen department is supervised by a deaconess who has shown a particular fitness for the position, and who continues in office indefinitely. She doles out supplies and supervises the first and second cooks, the "potato girl" and the "messer," as well as the breadmaker, the pastry cook and the brown bread girl.

All of these serve a term of one month in the kitchen and try to excel one another in the economical use of supplies and in the variety and toothsomeness of their food. The potato

girl is a young sister who prepares all the vegetables. Her lot is not an enviable one, as breakfast is at 6 and she must be in the kitchen at 4 in order to have her bushel of potatoes in the oven at 4:45. If the potatoes are not done by breakfast time the eldress says solemnly: "Brethren and sisters, we have no potatoes this morning. I suppose Sister Elizabeth overslept."

It is the duty of the "messer" to attend to those who for any reason cannot eat the regular food, preparing for them some extra dish whenever necessary, and as she has to keep in mind all the different tastes, her task is far from simple.

The "big" breakfast bell rings at ten minutes before 6, as a signal for all to assemble in the "waiting rooms"; at 6 the "small bell" sounds, the doors are opened, and, sisters on one side, brethren on the other, the "family" files quietly in. They kneel for a silent grace, then pull out their chairs, each with the right hand, and as soon as all are seated the meal begins. Each table holds sixteen persons, but the unit of the dining room is a "square," or four people, two on each side of the table. Every square forms an independent colony, with its own butter, salt, pepper, cream, bread and sugar; in the center of the square is a board on which are placed the oatmeal, potatoes, and codfish which form the usual breakfast, for in a Shaker Village both courses are put upon the table at once. The two sisters in charge of the dining room walk up and down to replenish any empty dish; the coffee, already mixed with hot cream, is brought in from the kitchen in large pitchers, and all eat as rapidly and silently as possible. There is no conversation, but a sister stands and reads extracts from the newspaper of the day before.

Each person is required to "clean up his plate," and as

CONTINUED

each one helps himself he is supposed to just take the amount he can eat; if he makes a mistake and puts too much on his plate he is obliged to finish it. Potato skins, bones and such substances as are absolutely uneatable are placed in "refuse bowls," one of which is provided for each square. As each finishes his meal he lays down knife and fork and the room grows very quiet. Finally the elder brother gives the signal by pushing back his chair, they kneel again for a silent thanksgiving, and file out to their day's work. Then the dining room sisters and the undercooks hurry to wash dishes and reset tables for the "second sitting" at 6:30. This consists of the old people and children, who have an extra half-hour to sleep, as they are not needed so early in the active work of the community. The cooks also eat at the second sitting.

There is the same ceremonial observance at the 12 o'clock dinner, but instead of the newspaper the eldress reads reports from other Shaker settlements, or on red-letter days, a short story or the account of some interesting event in the outside world. Dinner consists of meat, vegetables, puddings and pies.

Supper the sisters eat in absolute silence at half-past 5, and the brethren at 6. The usual supper is bread and butter, stewed fruit, hash, cheese, toast and tea or hot water with milk and sugar.

On Sunday there is boiled rice with maple syrup for breakfast. The dinner is baked beans, brown bread, pie with cheese, and tea. This is carefully planned in order that there may be as little cooking as possible on the Sabbath. At supper there is the weekly treat of cake. To make up for the lack of meat on Sunday, there usually is steak for dinner Monday, and on Tuesday there is a boiled dinner, with Indian pudding and cream.

When one considers the intelligence and the rivalry of the cooks, one begins to understand why the food, although perfectly simple, is so delicious. On the ordinary farm the choicest of everything goes to market, while in a Shaker Village the vegetables, cream, meats, etc. are used at home. The Shakers do not use pork in any form. [The Shaker's ban on pork lasted from 1841 to 1862.—Editor] Beef fat takes the place of lard, and as great quantities are needed it is purchased from the slaughterhouses of the neighboring city, as well as carefully saved from all home-killed beef. It is tried out under the direction of the deaconess, run into cakes and packed in barrels of brine for the winter supply.

The allowance of beef was one "creature" a month. The brethren planned to have it fat and ready to kill as the new cook began her term of office. In cold weather the meat could be stored in the ice house and used while fresh, but in hot weather a large part of it was made into "bacca," a delicious form of salted meat, the exact recipe for which is given later. In the fall half a dozen extra "creatures" were killed and the meat corned, for one hundred hungry persons cannot be fed for a whole month upon even the largest beef. There was veal in its season and chicken once or twice in the fall, as well as Thanksgiving and Christmas. During the summer the fishman came once a week and in the winter oyster stew was occasionally served for breakfast. Eggs were used freely when the hens could be persuaded to lay, at other times great economy prevailed. In the early days sheep were raised for wool as well as for food, so there was plenty of mutton and lamb,

CONTINUED

but this industry was given up some thirty years ago, as the dogs of the neighborhood killed and worried the flock continually.

In the early spring the boys went down to the meadows for cowslip greens, which are cooked like dandelions, but are more delicate in flavor. Dandelion greens the cooks gathered themselves, and during its season they would cut the asparagus at 4 A.M. to be cooked for breakfast or packed away for dinner. In the summer there was always an abundance of fresh vegetables, such as boiled beets, beans of all sorts, mashed turnips, carrots, parsnips and asparagus, most of them cooked in cream. One who has never tried it can have no idea how good vegetables are prepared in this way. Then there were salads of lettuce, cress, peppergrass, young onions and pusley (purslane), all eaten with a salad dressing made of one part vinegar to two of water, and enough molasses to sweeten. The vinegar being homemade was excessively strong, and so had to be diluted. The regular winter vegetables were packed away in cellars, and corn and beans were so skillfully dried that when cooked in the inevitable cream they could not be distinguished from fresh ones. Tomato was the only canned vegetable. Some white potatoes were taken to the city and exchanged for sweet ones. These were invariably boiled and accompanied by boats of "dopp gravy," made of thin cream slightly thickened with flour and butter and served very hot.

Pie with cheese was never absent from the dinner table, usually apple pie, sometimes squash or custard. The puddings were always of the simplest, rice, bread and tapioca being the stand-bys. A great deal of "sauce" was eaten, so the sisters had to prepare a tremendous amount of canned fruit, which was remarkably good, partly because they used less sugar than most cooks. Blueberries were dried to take the place of raisins. Cranberries were canned and barberries were put up in molasses, stems and all. They also had black and white raspberries and fancy currants, as well as melons of all sorts.

Shaker bread must be eaten to be appreciated. The sisters raise the hops and make their own yeast, so the bread is delightfully moist. It is usually made of graham or whole wheat flour, as they are considered more wholesome, but a small amount of fine flour is made up for those who cannnot eat the others. The sisters make their own butter, and most

CONTINUED

*delectable butter it is, except when it is scarce, then the pru-
dent supervisor puts in an extra amount of salt to make the
butter go farther. It does. They make three kinds of common
cheese, "cream," "three-milk," and "skim-milk." The first is
made of whole fresh milk, the second of three consecutive
milkings, the third of skim milk. This last is a leathery cheese,
but delicate in flavor and free from grease. Then they make
sage, Johnswort and tansy cheese, besides the cottage cheese.
Sour milk is used in cooking in order to save cream of tartar,
and great two-quart pitchers of skim milk are on the table at
every meal.*

*Long ago the Shakers considered real tea too expensive,
and so drank "liberty tea," made of a common herb which
they gathered and prepared themselves. It received that name
"because the ministry gave them liberty to drink it." In those
days they made a wonderfully palatable and wholesome coffee of roasted barley ground and sweetened with molasses.
Sometimes they would add a small amount of roasted carrot
to give the coffee a rich yellow color. There is still a quaint
custom in vogue of serving "strippings" with the morning
coffee. After the regular milking a sister would go out and
"strip" the udders of the cream which the milkers had left.
This was then heated and mixed with the coffee. I add some
especially valuable Shaker recipes:*

PICKLE FOR BACCA

*Pound down close in a barrel one hundred pounds of the
round of beef cut in ten-pound pieces, with a mixture of four
pounds sugar, two ounces saltpeter, two ounces soda bicar-
bonate, and four quarts table salt sprinkled under, over and
between. It will make brine without water. After one week, a*

piece of the top of the round, sliced and broiled, will be found tender and delicious. The bottom of the round, boiled till tender and sliced thin when cold, resembles ham, but is more choice in flavor.

SHAKER GRAPE CATSUP

Boil for one hour five pounds grapes, boiled and sifted, three pounds sugar, one pint cider vinegar, two tablespoons of all kinds of spice, one teaspoon black pepper and one teaspoon cayenne pepper. Served with meat this is excellent.

SHAKER DRIED APPLE SAUCE

Wash and soak over night one pound of sour dried apples. Add one half pound sugar, and boil twelve hours, adding water as needed. This makes a delicious red apple sauce.

SHAKER BAKED BEANS WITHOUT PORK

Soak one quart of medium pea beans over night or twelve hours, then parboil till the skin cracks when taken up on a spoon and exposed to the cool air. Put a beef bone with marrow into the pot, and fill with beans, add two teaspoons of salt, and water to cover. Bake slowly for twelve hours, adding more water as it evaporates. Before serving take off the hard beans on the top.

SHAKER VINEGAR SAUCE

Mix one teaspoon of flour into a paste with a little water. Add one cup water, one-half cup sugar, butter the size of a horse chestnut, and boil three minutes. The consistency should be that of thick cream. Flavor with vinegar to suit taste. Serve with Apple Cake.

NOTE: Originally published in *Good Housekeeping* magazine, 1905, by a Shaker Sister identified only as Sister Marcia.

VENISON MEAT LOAF

Michelle York, one of our waitresses, inspired this wonderful recipe. During New Hampshire's deer hunting season, she makes delicious venison meatball sandwiches with Fresh Tomato Sauce (page 163). For Christmas, she and her husband, Dan, gave me some fresh venison burger (see Note) from one of his hunting expeditions to try for myself.

My recipe is for a meat loaf, delicious served with mashed potatoes and glazed carrots. However, you can easily shape the meat into those wonderful meatballs Michelle can't offer enough praise about.

1½ pounds venison burger	**1 tablespoon**
1½ pounds ground beef	**Worcestershire sauce**
1 small onion, peeled and	**2 tablespoons chopped**
finely diced	**fresh parsley**
½ cup fresh bread crumbs	**1½ teaspoons salt**
3 large eggs, beaten	**½ teaspoon freshly ground**
1 tablespoon minced garlic	**pepper**

1. Preheat the oven to 350°F.

2. In a large bowl, combine all of the ingredients and mix well. Shape the meat into a loaf and place into a large loaf pan.

3. Bake for 50 to 60 minutes, basting occasionally with the natural drippings in the pan. Let the meat loaf sit for 5 to 10 minutes before serving.

SERVES 6 TO 8

NOTE: Venison burger is freshly ground venison with the addition of beef suet. The suet is added because the venison is very lean and dry. Venison is available at most specialty meat shops.

POULTRY

OUR FAMOUS BARBECUED CHICKEN

The Shakers loved a good barbecue with everyone pitching in, and old-fashioned community chicken barbecues are still very much alive and well in New Hampshire. Five times each year we fire up the sixteen-foot barbecue pit for our famous chicken dinner: barbecued chicken, chilled potato-egg salad (page 18), corn bread (page 52), and slices of watermelon.

We'd like to share with you the secret that keeps them coming back for more, year after year. It's this sauce, inspired by Emerson Moore, longtime friend of the Village and a twenty-five-year veteran of the community chicken barbecue. Thanks, Emerson!

BARBECUE SAUCE

½ cup (1 stick) unsalted butter
1 cup cider vinegar
1 tablespoon salt
½ cup water

1 teaspoon finely chopped garlic
1 tablespoon finely chopped shallots
1 sprig fresh parsley
1 sprig fresh tarragon

One 3½-pound chicken, split, or 4 boneless chicken breast halves

TO MAKE THE SAUCE

1. Combine all of the ingredients in a large saucepan. Bring the sauce to a boil over medium heat, turn off the heat, and let sit for 30 minutes. Strain the sauce, discarding the garlic, shallots, and herbs, and keep warm (see Note).

TO GRILL THE CHICKEN

2. Place 6 to 8 pieces of wood or charcoal to form a pyramid. Light the fire. (Do not use lighter fluid; the chemicals will spoil the sweet aroma of the fire.) When the fire gets rolling, after about 10 minutes, add more wood to build a big enough bed of coals. The fire must burn about 35 to 40 minutes before it's ready to start grilling. For boneless chicken breasts the coals should be red-hot with a light coating of ashes, and for half chickens or chicken pieces the coals should be allowed to cool a little, with a good coating of gray ashes, before grilling begins.

3. Baste the chickens frequently, the more often the better, with the sauce throughout the grilling process (see Note). Boneless breasts will take about 15 minutes, chicken parts with the bones will take about 20 to 30 minutes, and half chickens at least 30 to 35 minutes.

SERVES 2 TO 4

NOTE: If you are making the sauce ahead of time, reheat over low heat before using. The sauce may be made 3 days ahead of time and kept refrigerated, as can leftover sauce.

I prefer to use wood or virgin chunk charwood for our outdoor grilling. For chicken I recommend using either maple or mesquite, both of which give off a wonderful sweet aroma. If these woods or charwood are not readily available, use charcoal briquettes as a last resort. Maple and mesquite charcoal will work sufficiently, but avoid charcoal made with fillers and chemicals that give off unpleasant odors when burned.

To build the fire use an electric starter or newspaper. Figuring out how much wood you'll need to cook with can come only with experience. A simple guideline to remember is it's always better to have a fire that's a little too big than one that's a little too small. It's difficult to tell your guests that the fire died out before you could finish cooking.

ROAST SPRING CHICKEN WITH TARRAGON BUTTER

This is true Shaker simplicity at its finest. A young chicken is seasoned with fresh tarragon, garlic, and shallots and slowly roasted to juicy perfection.

1 tablespoon minced fresh tarragon	**2 tablespoons unsalted butter, at room**
½ teaspoon minced garlic	**temperature**
½ teaspoon minced shallots	**Salt and freshly ground**
1½ teaspoons fresh lemon juice	**pepper to taste**
	One 2½- to 3-pound fresh chicken

1. Preheat the oven to 375°F.

2. In a small bowl, combine the tarragon, garlic, shallots, lemon juice, and butter, and mix until well blended. Add salt and pepper to taste.

3. Rinse the chicken inside and out with cold water, and pat dry. Carefully separate the skin from the chicken and smear the flavored butter under the loosened skin of the chicken. Place the chicken on a roasting rack in a roasting pan.

4. Roast the chicken for 1 hour, or until the thigh juices run clear when pricked with a fork. Allow the chicken to sit for 10 minutes before carving.

SERVES 2 TO 4

BAKED CHICKEN LOAF

The Shakers were well aware of meat loaf's capacity for transforming inexpensive cuts of meat into satisfying, delicious meals. This is a nice alternative to traditional beef meat loaf. Serve it warm with Herbed Cream Gravy (page 83), mashed potatoes and glazed carrots, on toast as an open-faced sandwich, or chilled as a sandwich with Spicy Remoulade Sauce (page 164).

2 pounds ground chicken
1 pound ground pork
3 large eggs, beaten
½ cup fresh bread crumbs
2 tablespoons minced
  shallots
1 tablespoon minced garlic

1 tablespoon chopped
  fresh parsley
2 teaspoons poultry
  seasoning
2 teaspoons salt
½ teaspoon ground white
  pepper

1. Preheat the oven to 350°F.

2. In a large bowl, combine all of the ingredients together and mix well by hand. Shape the meat into a large loaf and turn it into a large loaf pan. Place the pan in a larger baking pan and fill the larger pan with 1 inch of hot water.

3. Bake for 1 to 1¼ hours, or until the loaf is firm to the touch. Cut the loaf into slices and serve hot, or chill the loaf and serve cold

SERVES 6 TO 8

HOME TOPICS

A Connecticut farmer mixes a teaspoonful of cayenne or red pepper with the food of his hens, which causes them to lay more eggs. In six months a flock of twenty-six hens laid 2,025 eggs. On two occasions when by the omission of pepper the daily product was 9, the use of the spice brought up the number to 13 or more a day. The fowls were fed on corn-meal in the morning and oats at night.

Fowls seem exceedingly grateful for the gift of cold water. They never swallow a drop of it without turning up their eyes to heaven.

THE SHAKER MANIFESTO   SEPTEMBER 1882

PANFRIED CHICKEN AND MAINE CRAB CAKES WITH MINTED TARTAR SAUCE

I love crab cakes made with fresh Maine (Rock) crabmeat. Unfortunately, many crab cakes taste more like bread cakes flavored with artificial crab. This recipe is a happy medium between economically practical and full crab flavor.

Also try these with Spicy Remoulade Sauce (page 164), or, for that really special occasion, serve these cakes with Native Corn and Lobster Sauce (page 93).

1 pound fresh ground chicken	¼ cup chopped scallions, including greens
18 ounces Maine crabmeat, picked over and well drained	1 tablespoon chopped fresh parsley
1 large egg	2 teaspoons salt
2 cups fresh bread crumbs	½ teaspoon freshly ground pepper
½ cup heavy cream	Vegetable oil for panfrying
1 tablespoon Dijon mustard	Minted Tartar Sauce (recipe follows)

1. In a large bowl, combine the ground chicken, crab, egg, ½ cup bread crumbs, cream, mustard, scallions, parsley, salt, and pepper, and mix until well blended.

2. Place the remaining 1½ cups bread crumbs in a large shallow bowl.

3. Form the mixture into 12 evenly shaped cakes and coat them in the bread crumbs, shaking off any excess.

4. In a large heavy frying pan, heat ⅛ inch of oil over medium heat. Panfry the cakes until golden brown on the underside, about 3 minutes, then flip and cook on the other side until golden brown, about 3 minutes more. Drain on paper towels. Serve 2 cakes per person with Minted Tartar Sauce.

SERVES 6

MINTED TARTAR SAUCE

2 cups mayonnaise
2 tablespoons chopped
  fresh spearmint
1 tablespoon chopped
  fresh parsley
½ cup sweet pickle relish,
  drained

1 tablespoon capers,
  drained and chopped
2 teaspoons minced
  shallots
1 teaspoon Dijon mustard
Salt and freshly ground
  pepper to taste
Sugar to taste, if necessary

1. In a large bowl, combine all of the ingredients and mix until well blended.

2. Refrigerate, covered, a minimum of 2 hours before serving. This will keep in the refrigerator up to 3 days.

MAKES APPROXIMATELY 2½ CUPS

HOME TOPICS

How true it is that, if we observe and remember, we can learn something of everyone we meet. A few days ago I learned from the poorest housekeeper I know something new to me—that salt added to the flour before the water, cn stirring paste for starch or gravy, would prevent the flour from forming into lumps. Of course I used to salt both gravy and starch, but I never observed the good results of adding the salt first.

THE SHAKER MANIFESTO   MARCH 1880

COUNTRY-FRIED CHICKEN WITH HERBED CREAM GRAVY

This dish, inspired by the Pleasant Hill, Kentucky, Shakers, is just as good served hot as it is on a picnic served cold. Soaking the chicken in buttermilk overnight intensifies the flavor and ensures tender, juicy meat. I use boneless and skinless chicken breasts instead of cut-up whole chickens.

The dish is served with a traditional fresh Herbed Cream Gravy. I think seasoned mashed potatoes are also a must!

4 boneless and skinless chicken breasts, halved
1 quart buttermilk
2 cups unbleached all-purpose flour
1 tablespoon salt
1 teaspoon freshly ground pepper
2 teaspoons onion powder
2 teaspoons garlic powder
2 teaspoons dried thyme
2 teaspoons ground dried sage
1 teaspoon dried sweet basil
Vegetable oil for frying
Herbed Cream Gravy (recipe follows)

1. In a large bowl, soak the chicken breasts in the buttermilk overnight, covered, in the refrigerator.

2. In another large bowl, thoroughly combine the flour, salt,

pepper, onion powder, garlic powder, thyme, sage, and basil.

3. In a large cast-iron frying pan, heat ½ inch of oil to 350°F. Remove the chicken from the buttermilk, shake off the excess, and dredge in the seasoned flour. Shake off the excess flour.

4. Fry up to 4 pieces of chicken at a time. Cover the pan and fry for 4 to 5 minutes on each side, reducing the heat if the chicken is browning too quickly. Remove the cooked chicken, drain on paper towels, and keep warm in a 200°F. oven. Serve the fried chicken with the Herbed Cream Gravy.

SERVES 8

HERBED CREAM GRAVY

This traditional cream gravy, seasoned with chopped fresh herbs, is a main staple in Shaker cooking. We serve it not only with Country-Fried Chicken but with chicken-fried steak, over mashed potatoes, anywhere a delicious, rich gravy is called for.

**3 tablespoons unsalted
butter
1 tablespoon minced
shallots
½ teaspoon minced garlic
3 tablespoons unbleached
all-purpose flour
2 cups chicken stock**

**1 cup heavy cream
3 tablespoons chopped
fresh herbs (such as
parsley, chives,
tarragon, thyme)
Salt and freshly ground
pepper to taste**

1. In a large heavy saucepan, melt the butter over medium-low heat. Add the shallots and garlic, and cook 2 to 3 minutes, without allowing them to color. Add the flour and stir to form a paste. Cook for 3 to 4 minutes, stirring, being careful not to allow the mixture to brown.

2. Stir in the stock until smooth. Stir over medium heat until the sauce thickens, about 5 to 7 minutes. Stir in the cream and herbs, and season with salt and pepper. Cook over medium heat until heated through and serve hot.

MAKES APPROXIMATELY 3 CUPS

ROAST DUCKLING WITH SHAKER SMOTHERED ONIONS

**4 ducklings (about 4 to 5
    pounds each)
½ cup fresh rosemary
    leaves**

**Kosher salt
Freshly ground pepper
Shaker Smothered Onions
    (recipe follows)**

1. Preheat the oven to 400°F.

2. Rinse the ducklings inside and out with cold water, and pat dry. Pierce the skin of the ducklings with a fork several times, which will help to release some of the fat during roasting.

3. Chop the rosemary leaves. Season the ducklings with kosher salt, pepper, and rosemary.

TO ROAST THE DUCKLINGS

4. Place the ducklings, breast side up, on a roasting rack in a large roasting pan. Place the pan in the oven, immediately reduce the oven temperature to 375°F., and roast for 20 minutes per pound for the average weight of the ducklings (e.g., if the average duckling weighs 4½ pounds, cook for 1½ hours). Allow the ducklings to sit for about 5 minutes before carving. Serve ½ duckling per person accompanied by Shaker Smothered Onions.

SERVES 8

VARIATION

For grilled duck breasts: Duck breasts are available at specialty food stores and butcher shops and are becoming more readily available in the freezer section at most supermarkets. Defrost the duck breasts according to the instructions on the package.

One 12-ounce boneless duck breast, split, serves 2 people. Season the breasts with salt and freshly ground pepper, and grill as you would a steak. Cook to desired doneness, about 5 minutes per side over medium coals for medium doneness. For a more in-depth description on grilling and building a fire, see page 76.

SHAKER SMOTHERED ONIONS

What's interesting about this recipe for smothered onions is that they're not only creamed but also flavored with local cider. They accompany duck, chicken, pork, and ham equally well.

8 cups thinly sliced
    Spanish onions
5 tablespoons unsalted
    butter
5 tablespoons unbleached
    all-purpose flour

2 cups chicken stock
½ cup fresh apple cider
1 cup heavy cream
Salt, freshly ground
    pepper, and grated
    nutmeg to taste

1. Bring a large saucepan filled with lightly salted water to a boil over medium heat. Add the onions and cook until they are tender, 8 to 10 minutes. Drain well.

2. In a large heavy saucepan, melt the butter over low heat. Add the flour, stirring to form a paste, and cook 2 to 3 minutes without allowing it to color. Add the chicken stock and cider, stirring until smooth. Cook over medium-low heat, stirring often, until the sauce thickens, about 5 minutes. Add the blanched onions and heavy cream, and simmer the sauce over medium-low heat for an additional 10 to 15 minutes. Season with salt, pepper, and grated nutmeg, and serve hot with roast or grilled duckling.

SERVES 8

THANKSGIVING IN A SHAKER VILLAGE Like every other Shaker feast the observance of Thanksgiving was governed by the most definite rules, and yet in some ways our manner of keeping the day was not unlike that of the "world's people." Like them we had divine service in the morning, and social diversions in the evening, and, as among them, the dinner was the chief consideration of the day. The feast really began with breakfast, for, in addition to the regular fare, we always had boiled rice with maple syrup and home-canned peaches or cherries. At ten o'clock everyone went to church, except the head cooks, whose presence in the kitchen was absolutely necessary. During the service the elder brother read first the president's proclamation and then the governor's; the deacons and trustees, who had charge of all the property and money, gave an account of the temporal blessings of the year, suitable hymns were sung and the meeting was closed by a special prayer of thanksgiving, offered silently while all knelt.

The dinner was at twelve, and here chicken took the place of the conventional turkey. These chickens had been selected and fattened for weeks before, and so important was it that they should be cooked exactly right that if an inexperienced cook was on duty, a more skillful one was appointed for the day. The menu was fricasseed chicken with cream gravy, boiled white potatoes, baked Hubbard squash, mashed turnips, ripe tomato pickles, mince and apple pies, cheese, bread and butter, milk and tea. The squash was intended to take the place of sweet potato, but to my mind the squash, properly prepared, is far superior to any sweet potato that I have ever eaten. The pies had been standing ready on the pantry shelves several hours, and happy indeed was the little girl who was sent on an errand there and could look or even sniff at these delicacies. Thanksgiving pies differed from all others in as much as dried blueberries usually took the place of raisins, but for this day "store plums" were purchased and were considered to be a great luxury. There were always some unlucky ones who were not well enough to eat mince pie, so a batch of "apple pies with plums" was baked for them. The cheese, of course, was homemade.

As soon as the meal was over every able-bodied person, man, woman and child, was armed with a pail, a mop or a broom, and the procession moved to the barns, sheds or mills, for all outbuildings were to be cleaned and put in perfect order before half-past four. Every cobweb was

CONTINUED

brushed down, every window washed, and every bit of rubbish burned or carted off. By thanksgiving time the crops were all harvested, so on that day the carts, plows and farming implements were carefully put away to be in readiness for the next season. This ceremonial of cleansing explains the neat and tidy appearance of all Shaker villages. Although brethren and sisters worked together on this day, the tasks were cleverly allotted by the deacons and deaconesses so that if a certain sister and brother were supposed to like each other they were placed as far apart as possible. The general system was to have the elderly sisters near the young brothers while the girls were helping the older men. The Shaker discipline was not relaxed for a single instant, and if a giddy young sister even glanced at one of the brethren she was sure to be marked by the watchful eye of Eldress Some One. At half-past four came the milking, at which the sisters always assisted, and the six o'clock supper did not differ in any way from the usual one.

The evening was devoted to a festivity known as "union meeting." At half-past seven, nine or ten sisters would go to visit three or four brethren in their sitting room (there are always more women than men in a settlement). They sat six feet apart in straight backed chairs, each with a huge checked handkerchief spread over the knees. These kerchiefs were woven by the Shakers themselves on purpose for such occasions and were an emblem of social intercourse. On this particular evening they were useful, too, for in them the sisters put the popcorn which the brethren were allowed to bestow on them in honor of the day. As a rule no giving of presents was tolerated. Then the deaconess came in to distribute "president apples," a remarkably large and fine variety, kept for this very purpose. If the supply was abundant the trustees would take some to town and exchange them for oranges, which were passed about at the same time and were considered a great treat. There was nothing as sinful as games or gossip, a few hymns were sung and there was some simple and labored conversation about the crops and the

CONTINUED

weather. At half-past eight the festivities came to an end, that all might keep the good old Shaker rule of being in bed by nine o'clock.

SHAKER FRICASSEED CHICKEN, THANKSGIVING STYLE

Cut up the chicken as for an ordinary fricassee, put in a kettle with a perforated stand at the bottom to prevent burning, use water enough to steam and cook one hour, then add your salt. When the meat is perfectly tender put it in the oven and brown thoroughly, then add rich cream to the gravy, thickening it with a little flour and butter, and seasonings to taste. Serve in deep dishes.

BAKED HUBBARD SQUASH

Wash a hard shelled Hubbard squash and cut into pieces large enough to handle with ease; it is impossible to make them of uniform size. Take out the seeds and pulp, being careful not to waste any of the good part. Bake like potatoes until a fork can pass through the meat easily. Serve in the shell and eat with butter and salt. If the squash is a nice one it will be mealy when it is done.

SHAKER MASHED TURNIPS

Pare and remove any bad spots, then boil and mash six white turnips. Drain thoroughly, add a half a cup of rich cream, butter the size of an egg, and salt and pepper to taste.

SHAKER THANKSGIVING DAY MINCE PIES

The crust for these Thanksgiving pies was much richer than that of the everyday kind. It was made as follows: Take one quart of flour, one teaspoon of salt, one cup of fresh beef drippings, one cup of cream, add water enough to make a dough. Roll out a bit of this mixture, spread with soft butter, sprinkle with flour, and roll up like jelly cake, cut off a portion, stand on end, heap on flour and roll out. This makes the flakes of the top crust. The lower crust is rolled out from the plain mixture.

To three quarts of sour apples, pared, cored and chopped, allow one quart of beef, boiled tender and chopped fine; if very lean put in a little butter. Add a pound of seeded and a pound of seedless raisins, one cup of grape jelly, or two of grape juice, two pounds of sugar, a tablespoon of salt, and cook all together until the apple is soft. When cool add two tablespoons of cinnamon, one each of ground cloves, ginger and allspice, and two grated nutmegs; the spice should be mixed together carefully before being added to the rest. If the mincemeat is not tart enough, flavor with a little boiled cider or the juice and grated rind of a lemon. More sugar or salt may be added if desired.

Bake the pies in a slow oven until the crust is a nice brown, both the top and bottom; this requires about forty minutes.

Appeared in *Good Housekeeping*, November 1905, unidentified author.

PANFRIED TURKEY CAKES WITH NATIVE CORN AND LOBSTER SAUCE

Around the holidays it becomes a challenge to find something new to do with leftover roast turkey. The Shakers responded to this challenge by mixing chopped turkey meat with a white sauce and creating tempting panfried cakes. This is my version, which I serve with corn and lobster sauce my personal favorite, for dinner.

4 tablespoons (½ stick) unsalted butter
2 tablespoons minced shallots
1 teaspoon minced garlic
4 tablespoons unbleached all-purpose flour
2 cups hot turkey stock, chicken stock, or milk

2 large eggs
1 large egg yolk
5 cups finely chopped roasted turkey
1 tablespoon chopped fresh parsley
Salt and freshly ground pepper to taste

BREADING
¾ cup unbleached all-purpose flour
2 large eggs beaten with 2 tablespoons milk

1 cup dry bread crumbs
Vegetable oil for frying
Native Corn and Lobster Sauce (recipe follows)

1. In a large heavy saucepan, melt the butter over low heat and cook the shallots and garlic for 2 to 3 minutes without allowing them to color. Add the flour and stir to form a paste. Cook over low heat for 5 minutes, stirring often, without allowing it to color. Slowly stir in the stock until smooth. Cook over medium-low heat until the sauce thickens, about 5 to 8 minutes, stirring often. Remove from the heat and cool for 15 minutes.

2. Stir in the eggs, egg yolk, turkey, and parsley, and mix well. Season with salt and pepper, and cool completely. The recipe may be made up to this point a day ahead and kept refrigerated.

TO MAKE THE CAKES

3. Place the flour, egg wash, and bread crumbs into 3 separate shallow bowls.

4. Form the mixture into 8 evenly shaped cakes. Dredge the cakes in the flour, dip in the egg wash, and coat in the bread crumbs, shaking the excess off.

5. To deep-fry the cakes, bring 2 inches of oil to 375°F. and fry the cakes for 4 to 5 minutes per side until golden brown. To panfry the cakes, coat a skillet lightly with oil and cook the cakes over medium heat for 4 to 5 minutes on each side. Drain on paper towels. Serve 2 cakes per person with Native Corn and Lobster Sauce.

SERVES 4 AS AN ENTREE OR 8 AS AN APPETIZER

NATIVE CORN AND LOBSTER SAUCE

This sauce is also wonderful with poached fish, Panfried Chicken and Maine Crab Cakes (page 80), grilled chicken, and so on.

3 tablespoons unsalted butter	1 cup corn kernels (preferably fresh)
2 tablespoons minced shallots	1 cup diced freshly cooked lobster meat
3 tablespoons unbleached all-purpose flour	1 cup light cream
2 cups lobster or chicken stock	1 tablespoon chopped fresh parsley
	Salt and freshly ground pepper

1. In a large heavy saucepan, melt the butter over medium-low heat. Add the shallots, cooking for 1 minute, without allowing them to color. Stir in the flour and cook for 2 to 3 minutes, stirring often, without allowing the mixture to color. Add the stock and cook until the sauce thickens, about 5 to 8 minutes, stirring often.

2. Add the corn, lobster meat, cream, and parsley. Cook until heated through. Season with salt and pepper, and serve hot.

MAKES APPROXIMATELY 4 CUPS

TURKEY CASHEW LOAF

Turkey has become increasingly popular in its many forms, avail-able in roasts, whole breasts, thighs, drumsticks, and ground tur-key. All of these convenient cuts make it easier for turkey to grace our dinner tables more often.

Here is just one more variation on the basic meat loaf. As with all meat loaves, this is great hot and equally delicious served up cold in a sandwich.

2 pounds ground turkey
  meat
1 pound ground pork
2 large eggs, beaten
½ cup fresh bread crumbs
¼ cup minced onions
1 teaspoon minced garlic
1 tablespoon poultry
  seasoning

Pinch of ground allspice
1 teaspoon Worcestershire
  sauce
2 teaspoons salt
½ teaspoon ground white
  pepper
½ cup toasted unsalted
  cashews, chopped

1. Preheat the oven to 350°F.

2. In a large bowl, combine all of the ingredients and mix well by hand. Shape the meat into a loaf and turn into a large loaf pan. Place the loaf pan in a larger baking pan and fill the larger pan with 1 inch of hot water.

3. Bake for 1 to 1¼ hours, or until the loaf is firm to the touch. Cut the loaf into slices and serve hot, or chill and serve cold.

SERVES 6 TO 8

SEAFOOD

CREAMED OYSTERS

Amazingly enough, oysters used to be not only plentiful but inexpensive. Twice a year the Canterbury Shakers would collect two barrels of oysters from the supply train and cook them in various dishes. A typical winter Shaker supper might be creamed oysters served over toasted corn bread or served simply with buttered toast.

4 tablespoons (½ stick) unsalted butter
¼ cup unbleached all-purpose flour
2½ cups milk
½ cup heavy cream
2 large egg yolks
2 cups shucked raw oysters with their liquor

½ teaspoon Worcestershire sauce
Pinch each of dried marjoram, basil, and chervil
½ cup mayonnaise
Salt and freshly ground pepper to taste

1. In a large heavy saucepan, melt the butter over medium-low heat. Add the flour and stir until a smooth paste is formed. Cook 2 to 3 minutes without allowing it to color. Add the milk and cream, stirring constantly, until heated through. Beat in the egg yolks and continue to cook over low heat, stirring until the sauce thickens, about 5 minutes.

2. Add the oysters with their liquor, Worcestershire sauce, and herbs, and cook for 5 minutes over low heat, stirring often.

3. Remove from the heat and stir in the mayonnaise. Season with salt and freshly ground pepper to taste. Serve immediately over squares of toasted corn bread or toast.

SERVES 4

PANFRIED HERB-CRUSTED FLOUNDER FILLETS

The success of this dish depends on the fresh stone-ground corn-meal, fresh herbs, and of course, fresh New England flounder fillets.

1 cup stone-ground yellow cornmeal (see Sources)	**Salt and freshly ground pepper to taste**
¼ cup unbleached all-purpose flour	**1 cup milk**
¼ cup grated Parmesan cheese	**8 fresh flounder fillets (8 ounces each)**
1 tablespoon chopped fresh parsley	**Vegetable oil for panfrying**
1 tablespoon minced fresh chives	**Lemon wedges**
	Tartar Sauce (page 164) or Spicy Remoulade Sauce (page 164)

1. In a shallow bowl, combine the cornmeal, flour, Parmesan, parsley, chives, salt, and pepper. Pour the milk into another shallow bowl.

2. Dip the flounder fillets in the milk, allow the excess to drip off, then dip the fillets into the seasoned cornmeal mixture, coating evenly. Shake excess coating off.

3. Heat approximately ⅛ inch of oil in a large frying pan over medium heat. Place as many fillets into the frying pan as fit without overcrowding. Fry approximately 2 to 3 minutes per side, or until golden brown. Drain on paper towels. Serve immediately with fresh lemon wedges, homemade Tartar Sauce, or Spicy Remoulade Sauce.

SERVES 4 TO 8

MAINE SHRIMP RAREBIT

Although rarebit is traditionally made with beer or ale, at The Creamery we substitute rich chicken stock. My version of this dish also includes Vermont sharp Cheddar cheese and two kinds of Maine shrimp, fresh and fruitwood smoked.

3 tablespoons unsalted
   butter
3 tablespoons unbleached
   all-purpose flour
2 cups chicken stock, plus
   more as needed
3 cups grated Vermont
   sharp Cheddar cheese
1 teaspoon Worcestershire
   sauce

1 tablespoon minced fresh
   chives
1 pound fresh Maine
   shrimp, peeled
½ pound smoked Maine
   shrimp (see Sources)
Salt and freshly ground
   pepper to taste
Biscuits, English muffins,
   or toast

1. In a large heavy saucepan, melt the butter over low heat. Stir in the flour and cook for 2 to 3 minutes, without allowing the roux to color, stirring constantly. Add 2 cups chicken stock and stir until the sauce is smooth and thick, about 5 to 8 minutes.

2. Add the grated cheese, Worcestershire sauce, and chives, stirring over medium-low heat until all of the cheese has melted, about 3 to 5 minutes. Add the fresh shrimp and cook, stirring often, until the shrimp are almost cooked through, about 4 to 5 minutes. Add the smoked shrimp and cook just until the shrimp are hot. Season with salt and freshly ground pepper. Serve hot over hot biscuits, toasted English muffin halves, or toast.

SERVES 6

POACHED SALMON WITH MINTED SWEET PEA CREAM

Like most true "Yankees," the Shakers often served boiled salmon with egg sauce, peas, and boiled potatoes on Independence Day. Here at The Creamery we started a new tradition a few years ago serving poached salmon fillet with minted pea sauce and boiled potatoes in parsley butter.

MINTED SWEET PEA CREAM

2 cups fresh sweet peas, washed

2 cups chicken stock

1 to 2 teaspoons minced fresh spearmint

½ cup light cream

Salt and freshly ground pepper to taste

4 to 6 cups fish stock (optional)

8 boned salmon fillets (8 ounces each)

TO MAKE THE SAUCE

1. In a saucepan, combine the peas, stock, and mint, and bring to a simmer over medium heat. Cook, stirring, for 20 to 30 minutes.

2. Carefully puree the mixture in a blender or food processor, then stir in the cream, and season with salt and freshly ground pepper to taste.

TO POACH THE SALMON

3. In a large pot, heat 2½ to 3 inches of fish stock or lightly salted water to a simmer over medium-low heat.

4. Place the salmon fillets in the water and poach the fish for approximately 8 minutes, keeping the poaching liquid at a simmer. The fillets will be firm to the touch when done. Remove the fillets and drain. Pat dry with paper towels. Serve on top of the Minted Sweet Pea Cream or napped with the sauce.

SERVES 8

POTATO-CRUSTED SALMON ON CREAMED MAINE CRABMEAT

This recipe was inspired by one of Sister Ethel's favorite comfort meals, creamed salmon on Pat Murphy's or canned salmon in white sauce served on baked jumbo white potatoes. Ethel said "Pat Murphy's" was a nickname given by a kitchen Sister for Irish potatoes.

Here I've reversed the original recipe and put the potatoes on the salmon, which is served on a bed of creamed fresh Maine crabmeat. The salmon is first panfried, then finished off in the oven.

3 eggs
¼ teaspoon minced garlic
2 tablespoons grated
   Parmesan cheese
1 teaspoon chopped fresh
   basil
1 teaspoon chopped fresh
   parsley
1 large Maine potato

Flour for dusting
8 boneless and skinless
   salmon fillets (6 to 8
   ounces each)
Salt and freshly ground
   pepper to taste
Vegetable oil for panfrying
Creamed Maine Crabmeat
   (recipe follows)

1. Preheat the oven to 400°F.

2. In a shallow bowl, blend the eggs, garlic, Parmesan, basil, and parsley to make an egg wash.

3. Peel and shred the potato with a hand grater into a bowl. Using your hands, squeeze out as much water as possible from the shredded potatoes.

4. Place the flour in a shallow bowl. Dust one side of the fillets with the flour, dip floured-side-down in the egg wash and then into the shredded potatoes. Season with salt and pepper.

5. Heat about ⅛ inch of oil in a large heavy frying pan over medium heat. Place the fillets, potato-side-down, in the pan and panfry until golden brown, about 2 to 3 minutes. Remove the fillets from the pan and transfer to a lightly oiled baking sheet, potato-side-up. Finish cooking the fillets in the oven, approximately 8 to 10 minutes.

6. To serve, place ½ cup Creamed Maine Crabmeat on each serving dish. Place a salmon fillet, potato side up, in the center of the creamed crabmeat. Serve immediately.

SERVES 8

CREAMED MAINE CRABMEAT

1 quart heavy cream
1 tablespoon Dijon
   mustard
2 tablespoons chopped
   scallions

12 ounces Maine crabmeat,
   drained well
   (approximately 2½ cups)
Salt and freshly ground
   pepper to taste

1. In a large heavy saucepan, reduce the cream over medium heat until 2½ cups remain, stirring often. This should take about 10 to 15 minutes.

2. Add the mustard, scallions, and crabmeat, and blend well, cooking until heated through. Season the sauce with salt and freshly ground pepper. Serve hot.

MAKES APPROXIMATELY 4 CUPS

PEPPERED BLUEFISH
POTATO CAKES

Anyone familiar with New England cookery has heard of salt cod breakfast cakes, a mixture of flaked salt cod and seasoned mashed potatoes shaped into cakes and panfried to a golden brown.

Here peppered bluefish is substituted for the salt cod, creating a new taste for this classic. They're not just for breakfast anymore!

3 pounds Maine potatoes
1½ pounds smoked
    peppered bluefish
    fillets, flaked (see
    Sources)
½ cup (1 stick) unsalted
    butter, at room
    temperature
5 large egg yolks
2 large hard-cooked eggs,
    peeled and chopped

2 tablespoons chopped
    fresh parsley
Salt and freshly ground
    pepper to taste
Bacon grease or vegetable
    oil for panfrying
Flour for dusting
Tartar Sauce (page 164) or
    Spicy Remoulade Sauce
    (page 164)

1. Peel and cube the potatoes. Bring a large pot of lightly salted water to a boil, and cook the potatoes until tender, about 20 to 25 minutes. Drain very well and allow to dry. In a large bowl, mash the potatoes and add the flaked bluefish, butter, egg yolks, chopped eggs, and parsley, and mix until well blended. Season with salt and freshly ground pepper.

2. Form the mixture into 16 evenly shaped cakes, approximately ½ cup each. Refrigerate the cakes, covered, at least 1 hour and up to 3 hours.

3. Heat ⅛ inch of bacon grease or vegetable oil in a large frying pan over medium heat. Dust the cakes with flour and panfry until lightly browned on the underside, about 1½ to 2 minutes, then flip once and cook for 1½ to 2 minutes more. Serve 2 cakes per person with Tartar Sauce or Spicy Remoulade Sauce.

SERVES 8

SISTER ETHEL'S
CHARBROILED TINKERS

*Breakfast was the most important meal for the Shakers, and a
hearty one at that, designed to give them sustenance for their
busy days. A typical breakfast entrée might be salt cod potato
cakes and hot oyster stew, and there was always apple pie to
complete the meal.*

*Sister Ethel's favorite breakfast was Tinkers, baby Atlantic
mackerel dipped in melted butter, charbroiled, and served with
fresh lemon, fried eggs, a rasher of crispy country-smoked bacon,
and boiled potatoes. A truly substantial meal!*

8 Tinker fillets (Atlantic mackerel)	**Salt and freshly ground pepper**
½ cup (1 stick) unsalted butter, melted	**1 lemon, quartered into wedges**

1. Preheat the broiler or light a charcoal fire.

2. Dip the fillets in the melted butter, season with salt and
pepper, and broil or grill. These will cook incredibly fast, about
1½ to 2 minutes per side. Be careful not to overcook them. Serve
2 fillets per person with fresh lemon.

SERVES 4

THE MANIFESTO The Shakers produced their own monthly informational periodical from 1871 to 1899, successively called *The Shaker, The Shaker and Shakeress, The Shaker Manifesto,* and *The Manifesto.* Despite name and location changes, first being published in Watervliet, New York, then New Lebanon, New York, and Canterbury, New Hampshire, each issue was consecutively numbered throughout its twenty-eight years of existence.

These periodicals are a great source for recipes, general household hints, and accounts of daily life at the different Shaker communities.

VEGETABLES

OUR OPINIONS OF FRUITS AND VEGETABLES

We have heretofore been favorably impressed with the Trophy *and* Canada Victor *tomatoes. Acknowledging these to be good still, we have proved this season that the* Acme *is superior to any other variety known to us. If there is a better, we would be glad to know it. We have tested the New Melon, The Surprise—and were disappointed at finding it inferior to the* Sill's Hybrid. *This latter, while not so juicy as the* Green-Fleshed Nutmeg, *is every way its superior, and as a universal Musk-melon, we should deem it unequaled.*

THE SHAKER MANIFESTO   NOVEMBER 1878

SAUTÉED ZUCCHINI AND CANTALOUPE WITH SPEARMINT

When asked what vegetables are synonymous with New Hampshire, zucchini is right up there at the top of the list. Everyone grows it, as did the Shakers, and ends up with too much of it, as did the Shakers. Inevitably gardeners ask the question, "What will I do with all this zucchini?" Here is one way to use the most common summer squash variety in a new and refreshing dish.

2 pounds zucchini, washed	2 tablespoons chopped
1 cantaloupe	fresh spearmint
6 tablespoons (¾ stick)	Salt and freshly ground
unsalted butter	pepper to taste
	Sugar to taste

1. Trim the ends of the zucchini and cut in half lengthwise. Cut the halves into ¼-inch-thick slices.

2. Peel and cube the melon or scoop into small balls.

3. In a large frying pan, melt the butter over medium heat. Increase the heat to medium-high and add the zucchini. Sauté, tossing for 2 to 3 minutes. Add the spearmint and melon, and sauté just until the melon is heated through. Season with salt, pepper, and sugar, if desired, and serve immediately.

SERVES 6 TO 8

BUTTERNUT SQUASH PUREE WITH CAPE COD CRANBERRIES

This recipe is a traditional Shaker dish served at Thanksgiving, when squash and cranberries are at peak season.

3½ pounds peeled and seeded butternut squash
One 12-ounce bag fresh cranberries, washed and picked over

½ cup (1 stick) unsalted butter
½ cup light brown sugar
Salt and ground white pepper to taste

1. Cut the peeled and seeded squash into 1-inch cubes.

2. Heat a large pot of lightly salted water to a boil over medium heat. Add the squash and cook for 15 minutes. Add the cranberries and continue to cook until the squash is very tender and the cranberries burst, about 10 minutes. Drain the squash and cranberries well.

3. Combine the squash, cranberries, butter, and brown sugar in the bowl of an electric mixer or food processor, and process until the mixture is pureed. Season with salt and white pepper, and serve hot.

SERVES 6 TO 8

SHAKER ALABASTER

I learned this dish of mashed potatoes and mashed turnips swirled together from the Sisters at the Village. Traditionally the dish includes no butter so as not to taint the natural pure white color of the vegetables. We serve Shaker Alabaster as an accompaniment to roast duckling and pot roast.

**1½ pounds Maine potatoes,
    peeled and quartered
1½ pounds white turnips,
    peeled and quartered**

**1½ cups heavy cream
Salt and white pepper
    to taste**

1. Heat 2 separate pots of lightly salted water to a boil. Cook the turnips in one pot and the potatoes in the other over medium heat until very tender, about 20 to 30 minutes. Drain well.

2. In 2 separate large bowls, mash the turnips and potatoes separately, each with ¾ cup heavy cream. Season with salt and white pepper.

3. Gently swirl the mashed turnips into the mashed potatoes and serve hot.

SERVES 6 TO 8

SPRING-DUG PARSNIPS

Parsnips are one of those vegetables that are not that popular outside New England, which is a shame as they are quite delicious and versatile. They are harvested in late fall and early spring. I prefer parsnips harvested in the early spring, which have been underground all winter, allowing their natural starches to convert to sugar and thereby producing a sweeter and somewhat spicier parsnip.

**4 pounds parsnips,
    preferably spring-dug
1 cup light cream**

**½ cup (1 stick) unsalted
    butter
Salt and ground white
    pepper to taste**

1. Heat a large pot of lightly salted water to a boil.

2. Peel and trim the parsnips. Cut them into 1-inch pieces. Add the parsnips to the boiling water and cook until very tender, about 25 minutes. Drain the parsnips well.

3. In a saucepan, heat the cream and butter over low heat until the butter is melted. Place the parsnips in the bowl of an electric mixer or food processor, and puree, adding the warm cream mixture a little at a time until it is all incorporated. Season with salt and white pepper, and serve hot.

SERVES 6 TO 8

A NEW FRUIT

A novel freak of nature was lately shown us by D. A. Buckingham, the venerable elder of Watervliet Society at Shakers, N.Y. It was about eighteen inches of grape vine, of Delaware variety, upon which he had, early in the spring, stuck an early Rose potato to prevent the vine from bleeding. The vine had grown four or five feet from the ground, and the potato had sprouted, and maintaining its vitality had grown nearly all over its surface, curious mongrel fruit, resembling equally well, potatoes and grapes, perhaps to the number of fifty. The green foliage around the fruit was equally mixed, half and half of potato leaves and grape leaves. It is the purpose of the Elder, we learn, to try his hand at bringing into use, either a potato with a grape skin or a grape as large as a potato; and we wish him success in either case.

THE SHAKER MANIFESTO   DECEMBER 1878

FRIED POTATO BALLS IN SMOKED BACON, SCALLION, AND PECAN BUTTER

This presentation offers a change from the more common methods of preparing America's favorite starch. The Shakers grew acres and acres of potatoes, using them in a myriad of ways.

The Smoked Bacon, Scallion, and Pecan Butter is also great on grilled fish, chicken, or tossed with your favorite fresh pasta.

6 large Maine or other boiling potatoes (about 2 pounds)

¼ cup Smoked Bacon, Scallion, and Pecan Butter (recipe follows)
Salt and freshly ground pepper to taste

1. Heat a large pot of lightly salted water to a boil. Meanwhile, peel the potatoes.

2. Using a melon baller, scoop small balls out of the potatoes and cook the potato balls in the boiling water just until tender, about 5 minutes. Drain well.

3. In a large frying pan, melt the smoked bacon butter over medium heat. Add the potato balls and cook until lightly browned, about 2½ to 3 minutes. Shake the pan occasionally to brown the potatoes evenly. Season with salt and pepper, and serve hot.

SERVES 4 TO 6

SMOKED BACON, SCALLION, AND PECAN BUTTER

½ **pound smoked bacon, diced (see Sources)**

¾ **cup (1½ sticks) unsalted butter**

¼ **cup sliced scallions, including greens**

¼ **cup pecan pieces**

Salt and freshly ground pepper to taste

1. In a heavy frying pan, cook the bacon over medium heat until crisp, about 8 minutes. Drain off the grease.

2. Combine the cooked bacon, butter, scallions, and pecans in the bowl of a food processor. Process until the ingredients are well blended. Scrape down the sides of the bowl with a rubber spatula once or twice. Season the mixture with salt and pepper.

3. Shape the butter into a cylinder on a piece of wax paper about 1 inch in diameter, and roll up tightly. Refrigerate or freeze until needed.

MAKES ABOUT 1¼ CUPS

MASHED POTATOES WITH SCALLIONS AND PARMESAN CHEESE

There's something about mashed potatoes that makes me feel welcome and at home when I see them on the dinner table.

We serve mashed potatoes at The Creamery almost every day we are open. Mashed potatoes are a very important part of a Shaker meal, perfect for soaking up all the sauces the Shakers loved so much. Most of the dishes would be incomplete without them.

6 large Maine or russet potatoes, about 2 pounds	**½ cup sliced scallions, including some greens**
½ cup (1 stick) unsalted butter	**½ cup grated Parmesan cheese**
1 tablespoon minced garlic	**Salt and freshly ground pepper to taste**
1 cup milk	

1. Heat a large pot of lightly salted water to a boil over medium heat.

2. Peel and quarter the potatoes, and cook in the boiling water until tender, about 30 minutes. Drain well.

3. In a saucepan, melt the butter over medium-low heat, add the garlic, and cook 1 to 2 minutes; do not allow to brown. Add the milk and continue to cook until hot. Remove from the heat.

4. In a large bowl, mash the potatoes and beat in the buttermilk mixture, scallions, and Parmesan cheese. Season with salt and pepper, and serve hot.

SERVES 4 TO 6

HOME TOPICS

A small piece of charcoal put into the pot of boiling cabbage removes the smell.

SMOKED BACON AND CHIVE POTATO PANCAKES

Next to seasoned mashed potatoes this is by far my favorite potato recipe. These pancakes are great at breakfast with eggs and sausage, or at dinner with roast pork or duckling. No matter when you serve them, don't forget the Chunky Applesauce (page 165).

4 cups peeled and grated
   Idaho or russet potatoes
1 small onion, peeled and
   finely diced
1 tablespoon minced fresh
   chives
½ cup cooked diced
   smoked bacon or
   smoked ham

3 large eggs
3 tablespoons unbleached
   all-purpose flour
Salt and freshly ground
   pepper to taste
Vegetable oil for panfrying

TO MAKE THE BATTER

1. In a large bowl, combine the grated potatoes, onion, chives, and bacon.

2. In a small bowl, combine the eggs and flour, and mix until smooth. Stir into the potato mixture and mix until well blended. Season with salt and pepper.

TO COOK THE PANCAKES

3. In a large heavy frying pan, heat about ⅛ inch of oil over medium heat. Drop the batter (2 tablespoons at a time, lightly pressing) to form 3-inch-round cakes and panfry on both sides until lightly browned and crisp, about 4 minutes on each side. Repeat until all of the mixture has been used, keeping the cooked pancakes hot in a 200°F. oven. Serve hot with applesauce or sour cream.

MAKES 8 PANCAKES

VARIATION

For Sweet Potato Pancakes, substitute 2 cups peeled and grated sweet potatoes for 2 cups grated Idaho or russet potatoes.

POTATO CROQUETTES

Potato croquettes were more or less a dish devised to use up leftover mashed potatoes. Not so at The Creamery. We actually go out of our way and make them fresh. They offer a delightful change of pace from the more common preparations.

Two or three croquettes served with cream gravy, a hot biscuit, and some fresh vegetables make a nice lunch.

**4 medium Idaho or russet
potatoes (about 1½
pounds), peeled
and quartered
2 tablespoons (¼ stick)
unsalted butter, at room
temperature
4 large egg yolks
½ cup sliced scallions,
including greens
1 cup finely diced smoked
ham**

**¼ cup grated Parmesan
cheese
Salt and freshly ground
pepper to taste
Vegetable oil for frying
½ cup unbleached all-
purpose flour
2 large eggs beaten with
2 tablespoons milk
1¼ cups dried bread crumbs**

1. Heat a large pot of lightly salted water to a boil. Add the potatoes to the water and cook until very tender, about 20 to 30 minutes. Drain well, and allow to dry.

2. Mash the potatoes in a mixing bowl or put them through a food mill. Beat in the butter, egg yolks, scallions, ham, and Parmesan, mixing well. Season with salt and pepper. Shape the potato mixture into 8 even portions (round balls, cylinders, or patties) and chill, covered, for at least 2 hours.

3. Heat 2 inches of oil to 375°F. in a large heavy saucepan, over medium heat.

4. Place the flour, egg wash, and bread crumbs in 3 separate shallow bowls. Lightly coat the croquettes with the flour, dip in the egg wash, and coat with the bread crumbs. Deep-fry until golden brown on all sides, about 3 to 4 minutes in all. Drain on paper towels and serve hot.

MAKES 8 CROQUETTES

SWEET POTATO PUREE

The Shakers used sweet potatoes in lots of preparations that varied depending on the region of each community. In Pleasant Hill, Kentucky, they were favored by the Shakers in a pie.

For this recipe I prefer the sweeter, orange potato that's most often confused with the yam. This variety lends itself well to blending with fruits, such as raisins, apricots, and currants. The surprise taste in this recipe is from the addition of a banana.

6 large sweet potatoes
(about 2 pounds)
1 large ripe banana,
peeled
4 tablespoons (½ stick)
unsalted butter, at room
temperature

2 tablespoons light
brown sugar
1 cup warm milk
Salt and freshly ground
pepper to taste

1. Heat a large pot of lightly salted water to a boil.

2. Cook the potatoes in their skins about 40 minutes, or until tender. Drain. When the potatoes are cool enough to handle, peel them.

3. Combine the potatoes, banana, butter, brown sugar, and milk in the bowl of a food processor. Process into a smooth puree. Season with salt and pepper, and serve hot.

SERVES 4 TO 6

CANDIED POTATOES

This is another very simple Shaker-style potato dish. When potatoes are sautéed in caramelized sugar until they turn golden brown, I don't have any trouble getting even the finickiest kids to eat their vegetables.

3 pounds Idaho or russet
   potatoes, peeled and cut
   into 1-inch cubes
1 cup sugar
½ cup (1 stick) unsalted
   butter

2 tablespoons chopped
   fresh parsley
Salt and freshly ground
   pepper to taste

1. Heat a large pot of lightly salted water to a boil. Add the potatoes and cook just until they are tender, about 8 to 10 minutes. Drain well.

2. In a large heavy frying pan, melt the sugar over medium heat, watching that it doesn't burn. When the sugar starts to caramelize (brown), add the potatoes and butter. Sauté until the potatoes are soft and golden brown. Add the parsley, and season with salt and pepper. Serve immediately.

SERVES 6 TO 8

CREAMSICLE CARROTS

Eldress Bertha always stressed "to take the ordinary and make it extraordinary in everything that you do." With this in mind, I reworked their basic recipe of carrots baked in brown sugar and orange juice. I called this recipe Creamsicle Carrots because when all of the individual ingredients come together, the taste is reminiscent of that childhood ice cream treat.

1 cup orange juice
   concentrate
½ cup heavy cream
2 tablespoons light brown
   sugar

2 tablespoons minced fresh
   dill
3 pounds carrots, peeled
Salt and freshly ground
   pepper to taste

1. In a heavy saucepan, combine the orange juice concentrate, cream, brown sugar, and dill, and heat to a boil over medium heat. Simmer until reduced by about one-third.

2. Meanwhile trim and slice the carrots ¼ inch thick. Cook the carrots in a large pot of lightly salted water until tender, about 5 to 6 minutes. Drain well.

3. In a large heavy skillet, combine the carrots and the sauce. Cook over high heat until the carrots are glazed and fully cooked, tossing often. Season with salt and pepper, and serve hot.

SERVES 8

TOMATO HONEY GLAZED CARROTS

This recipe is a variation on an unusual glazed carrot recipe from the kitchen at Enfield Shaker Village, Connecticut.

3 pounds carrots, peeled
½ cup ketchup
½ cup honey
1 tablespoon chopped
  fresh basil
1 tablespoon chopped
  fresh parsley
4 tablespoons (½ stick)
  unsalted butter
Salt and freshly ground
  pepper to taste

1. Heat a large pot of lightly salted water to a boil. Meanwhile trim and cut the carrots into ¼-inch-thick slices. Cook the carrots in the boiling water, about 10 minutes. Drain well.

2. In a saucepan, combine the ketchup, honey, basil, and parsley. Cook over low heat until warm.

3. In a large skillet, melt the butter over medium heat. Add the carrots and increase the heat to high. Add the glaze and toss to coat the carrots evenly. Cook 2 to 3 minutes, or until the carrots are cooked through and glazed. Season with salt and pepper, and serve hot.

SERVES 8

SHAKER VEGETABLES Fruits and vegetables were a main staple of the Shaker diet. Several orchards of peaches, pears, quinces, cherries, and apples and acres upon acres of vegetables (carrots, onions, corn, potatoes, lettuce, squashes, beans, tomatoes, and cucumbers) were served fresh daily and canned and pickled for the winter months.

The Shakers are credited with the development of several varieties of fruits and vegetables: Northern Muscadine Grape, Union Village Grape, Mount Lebanon Grape, Wachusett Blackberry, Mountain Seedling Gooseberry, Austin Seedling Strawberry, Shaker Potato, Shaker Early Sweet Corn, Grape Potato, Shaker Tea, a variety of Oswego tea, and Shaker Plum.

Today Dan Holmes tends to the vegetable gardens that supply the restaurant with fresh produce that is harvested daily. Early each morning Dan and I get together to discuss what's ready to be harvested. It's wonderful—within minutes of being harvested the produce is being served to the lunch guests! We still grow the variety the Shakers once grew: eight varieties of leaf lettuce, four varieties of tomatoes; three varieties of beets, onions, and cucumbers; three varieties of potatoes, summer and winter squashes; and so on, just not in the large quantities. The Shakers once owned a plot of land near downtown Concord, New Hampshire, where they farmed potatoes. In 1939 the Village records state twenty-five acres of potatoes were planted. That's a lot of potatoes!

CORN AND SMOKED CHEDDAR CHEESE PUDDING

Corn pudding was typically found on the Shakers' breakfast table rather than the dinner table, but however you choose to serve it, it makes a delightful addition to any meal.

2 cups milk	**7 large eggs, beaten**
¼ cup sugar	**½ cup sliced scallions,**
1½ cups grated smoked	**including greens**
Cheddar cheese	**4 to 5 dashes hot pepper**
2 cups cream-style corn	**sauce**
2 cups corn kernels	**Salt to taste**

1. Preheat the oven to 325°F. Butter a 2-quart casserole dish.

2. In a saucepan, scald the milk and sugar. Add the cheese, stirring over medium-low heat until melted. Pour into a blender or food processor and process until smooth.

3. In a large bowl, combine the cream-style corn, corn kernels, eggs, and scallions, and beat until very well blended. Carefully and slowly stir in the scalded milk mixture. Add the pepper sauce and season with salt. Pour into the prepared casserole dish.

4. Place the casserole dish in a larger baking pan. Fill the larger pan with about 1 inch of hot water. Bake for 30 to 40 minutes, or until the pudding is set (when a toothpick inserted in the center comes out clean).

SERVES 6 TO 8

FIDDLEHEAD FERN SAUTÉ

Next to spring-dug parsnips, fiddleheads are the first vegetables of the new year and a delicious reminder that spring is on the way. They're often hard to find, growing only in the wild with a very short season, but they're worth seeking out.

Of the four edible ferns, Shield, Ostrich, Lady, and Cinnamon, the Ostrich fern is the most commonly available.

2 pounds fiddlehead ferns
½ cup (1 stick) unsalted butter
2 tablespoons minced garlic
2 tablespoons minced shallots
1 to 2 tablespoons fresh lemon juice
Salt and freshly ground pepper to taste

1. Heat a large pot of lightly salted water to a boil.

2. Meanwhile, pick over the ferns, removing the paperlike brown membrane, and cut off the ends of the stems. Blanch the ferns in boiling water for 1 minute, then drain. Rinse under cold water and drain again.

3. In a large skillet, melt the butter over medium-high heat. Add the garlic and shallots, and cook for 20 to 30 seconds, just until aromatic. Add the ferns and sauté for 1½ to 2 minutes. Season with the lemon juice, salt, and pepper. Serve immediately.

SERVES 6 TO 8

BEAN HOLE BEAN BAKE A couple of times each year, with the help of Flander's Bean Hole Beans (see Sources), we serve an old-fashioned bean hole bean dinner, a time-honored method learned from native Indians who baked beans in animal hides with bear fat and maple sugar in underground pits. The festivities start the day before, parboiling beans, cutting onions and salt pork, and getting the fire started. The fire is made in a large fieldstone-lined pit measuring twelve feet in length, four feet wide, and four feet deep. An average of 1½ to 2 cords of wood are burned down, yielding a good one-foot-deep bed of ash and coals. Each of the four iron kettles are filled with salt pork, beans, onions, molasses, spices, and water, tightly covered, and gently lowered into the coals. The pit is then covered and eight to twelve inches of loam is piled on top as insulation. The beans slow-cook underground overnight for a period of about sixteen hours. At noontime the pit is unearthed, and the bean kettles are carefully lifted from the pit using a Horn beam and six hungry men. Each pot is capable of serving 250 hungry visitors. The meal is rounded out with country smoked ham, creamy coleslaw, orange poppy corn bread, and a slice of watermelon. It's truly a memorable meal and event to witness firsthand.

SHAKER BRICK-OVEN BAKED BEANS Slow-baked beans were a staple food of the Shakers for many years. In the early 1930s the Shaker kitchen Sisters began to sell their beans, steamed brown bread, and a variety of pickles to neighbors and within no time at all they were making weekly trips into the city of Concord. They would sell right from the back of a truck, equipped with a customized cap, a replica of the wood-fired brick oven in which the beans were baked. The unique wood-fired oven, a large Shaker-made brick box with four revolving circular shelves, is said to have been designed by Sister Emeline Hart (1834–1914), originally from Enfield Shaker Village. The oven was built in the 1820 bakery room in 1878 and allowed for numerous items to be baked at one time. Eldress Bertha recalls twenty-four jumbo bean pots being slow-baked overnight in the brick oven at once while Sister Ethel recalls the oven being loaded with sixty loaves of bread at a time, quite an impressive oven for the times.

During the Shakers' ban on pork products (1841–1862) beef suet or butter was used as a substitute for salt pork in the making of the beans. When I first came to the Village in 1988 the sisters were still abstaining from using salt pork in the beans. A stick of butter was stirred into the beans after they were baked. Today we bake beans and steam brown bread almost on a daily basis at The Creamery. They are just as popular with guests today, who take them home by the quarts with a loaf of steamed brown bread, as they were with their original clientele that began in the 1930s.

OUR VERSION OF SHAKER BAKED BEANS

1 pound navy beans,
washed and picked over
½ pound salt pork or
smoked slab bacon,
thinly sliced
1 medium onion, peeled
and diced
½ cup dried apples,
chopped fine (see Note)

1 tablespoon Coleman's
dry mustard
1 teaspoon baking soda
1 teaspoon freshly ground
pepper
2 tablespoons black strap
molasses (see Note)
½ cup maple syrup,
preferably dark amber
or grade B

1. Soak the beans overnight in cold water to cover. Drain the beans and cook them in fresh water over medium heat, simmering just until tender, about 30 minutes. Drain well.

2. Preheat the oven to 250°F.

3. In a large bean crock (see Sources), line the sides and bottom of the pot with the salt pork or bacon. Add the beans to the pot.

4. In a large saucepan, heat 1 quart water to a boil. In another large saucepan, combine the onion, dried apples, mustard, baking soda, pepper, molasses, maple syrup, and 2 cups of water. Mix well over low heat until hot. Pour the mixture over the beans and add enough boiling water to cover the beans. Cover the pot and bake for 3 to 4 hours, checking periodically to make sure the water level stays about even with the top of the beans, adding more, if necessary. Remove the cover for the last half hour of baking.

5. Stir well and serve hot with country-smoked ham (page 58) and steamed brown bread (page 48).

SERVES 6 TO 8

NOTE: Dried apples and black strap molasses are available at your local natural food store.

HERBED RICE PILAF

2 tablespoons (¼ stick)
unsalted butter
1 small onion, peeled and
finely diced
1 bay leaf
2 cups long-grain rice

3 cups chicken stock
2 teaspoons chopped fresh
tarragon or thyme
1 tablespoon chopped
fresh parsley
Salt and freshly ground
pepper to taste

1. Preheat the oven to 400°F.

2. In a large casserole, melt the butter over medium heat. Add the onion and bay leaf and sauté for 2 to 3 minutes. Add the rice, stirring to coat it with butter. Add the stock and bring to a simmer, then cover and cook in the oven for 20 minutes. Add the tarragon and parsley and fluff the rice with a fork. Remove the bay leaf. Season with salt and pepper, and serve hot.

SERVES 6

SISTER REBECCA'S COLD PICKLE

This recipe is from Sister Rebecca Hathaway, who became a Kitchen Deaconess at Canterbury Shaker Village in 1912.

16 ripe tomatoes

4 green peppers (2 hot, 2 sweet)

4 good-sized onions

1 cup sugar

1 cup vinegar

½ cup salt

—Run the tomatoes, peppers, and onions through a food chopper. Add the sugar, vinegar, and salt, and mix well.

MAKES ABOUT 1½ QUARTS

DESSERTS

WILD BLUEBERRY COBBLER WITH WHIPPED CREAM BISCUIT TOPPING AND LEMON–POPPY SEED– SOUR CREAM ICE CREAM

A decadent combination of some very popular Shaker creations.

WHIPPED CREAM BISCUIT TOPPING

2 cups pastry flour or
    unbleached all-purpose
    flour
2 tablespoons baking
    powder

1 teaspoon salt
¼ cup sugar
1 teaspoon lemon zest
1½ cups heavy cream

COBBLER

3 pints wild blueberries,
    picked over and washed
½ cup sugar, plus extra for
    sprinkling

1 teaspoon lemon zest
2 tablespoons minute
    tapioca

Lemon–Poppy Seed–
    Sour Cream Ice Cream
    (page 151) or whipped
    cream

TO PREPARE THE BISCUIT TOPPING

1. In a large bowl, sift together the flour, baking powder, salt, sugar, and zest. In another bowl, whip the heavy cream until it forms soft peaks. Stir the whipped cream into the flour mixture with a fork. When the dough starts to come together, knead by hand 8 to 10 times. Cover and refrigerate for 30 minutes.

TO MAKE THE COBBLER

2. In a large bowl, toss the blueberries with the sugar, lemon zest, and tapioca. Pour the mixture into a lightly greased 2-quart square baking dish.

TO ASSEMBLE THE COBBLER

3. Preheat the oven to 350°F.

4. Roll out the biscuit dough on a lightly floured surface ½ inch thick. With a floured 2½-inch-round biscuit cutter, cut out 9 biscuits.

5. Top the blueberry mixture with the biscuits, making 3 rows of 3. Sprinkle the biscuit tops with the additional sugar.

6. Bake the cobbler in the oven for 30 minutes, or until the biscuits are lightly browned. Allow the cobbler to cool for 15 to 20 minutes before serving. Serve warm with Lemon–Poppy Seed–Sour Cream Ice Cream or with whipped cream.

SERVES 9

SHAKER BROWN BETTY

Butter a deep pudding dish and place a layer of finely chopped apples in the bottom. Then add a layer of very fine bread crumbs and sprinkle with sugar and spice. Add a little butter, then another layer of apples and so on until the dish is filled. The top layer should be crumbs seasoned to taste. Bake in a moderate oven until quite brown, and serve with sweetened cream or hard sauce.

SISTER EDITH GREEN   1896

CHOCOLATE MINT CHEESECAKE WITH FRESH BERRY SYRUP

Chocolate mint, a special variety of mint, is my favorite variety for baking. When crumbled in your hand and sniffed, it reminds you of chocolate peppermint patties. The Shakers used to grow five varieties of mint: apple, peppermint, mountain, lemon, chocolate, and spearmint.

I've used this mint to flavor ice creams, dessert sauces, puddings, and now cheesecake. This particular recipe pays tribute to Eldress Bertha Lindsay, who throughout her entire life performed jobs such as stripping the chocolate mint for drying, a harvest tradition of the Shakers for more than 200 years.

CRUST

1½ cups chocolate wafer
    crumbs
¼ cup sugar

2 tablespoons (¼ stick)
    unsalted butter, at room
    temperature

FILLING

2 pounds cream cheese
1¾ cups sugar
5 large eggs
2 large egg yolks

2 teaspoons vanilla extract
¼ cup chopped fresh
    chocolate mint

Fresh Berry Syrup
   (page 155)

TO MAKE THE CRUST

1. Preheat the oven to 375°F.

2. Combine the wafer crumbs, sugar, and butter in a small bowl. Using your hands, combine the mixture, then press evenly into the bottom of a lightly buttered 10-inch springform pan. Refrigerate, covered, until needed.

TO MAKE THE FILLING

3. In a large bowl, mix the cream cheese and sugar with an electric blender on low speed until no lumps remain. Add the eggs and yolks one at a time, scraping down the bowl after each addition. Blend in the vanilla and mint. Let the batter rest for 30 minutes, covered, in the refrigerator.

4. Strain the batter into the prepared pan and bake for 1¼ hours, or until the cake is firm. Turn off the oven, leave the oven door ajar, and allow the cheesecake to sit in the oven for 1 more hour. Remove the cheesecake and cool completely on a wire rack. Unmold the cheesecake and serve with Fresh Berry Syrup, preferably made with raspberries.

MAKES ONE 10-INCH CAKE

POTATO CHIP COOKIES

I know what you're thinking: "Potato Chip Cookies?" This recipe was shared with us by our last Eldress and dear friend, Bertha Lindsay.
    All I can say is, try them, you'll like them!

2 cups unbleached all-purpose flour	1 cup chopped dates or raisins
½ teaspoon salt	1 cup granulated sugar
1 teaspoon baking soda	1 cup light brown sugar
2 cups crushed potato chips	1 cup (2 sticks) unsalted butter, softened
2 cups oatmeal	2 large eggs, well beaten
1 cup chopped nuts	

1. Preheat the oven to 375°F.
2. Sift the flour, salt, and baking soda into a large bowl, and mix in the crushed potato chips, oatmeal, nuts, and dates.
3. In a large bowl, cream the sugar, brown sugar, and butter until smooth. Slowly blend in the beaten eggs.
4. Gently mix in the sifted dry ingredients to form a dough, being careful not to overmix. Drop the dough by tablespoons onto a greased baking sheet. Bake the cookies for 10 to 15 minutes, or until lightly golden brown, and cool on a wire rack.

MAKES APPROXIMATELY 2½ DOZEN COOKIES

CHOCOLATE POUND CAKE

*This cake, from Hancock Shaker Village, Massachusetts, was tra-
ditionally baked in a Sally Lunn–type pan, but here it's made in
a bundt cake pan. The center can be filled with whipped cream
and shaved chocolate, or slices can be served with chocolate sauce
and ice cream or with fresh fruit.*

1 cup (2 sticks) unsalted butter	½ cup cocoa powder
½ cup vegetable shortening or lard	½ teaspoon baking powder
	¼ teaspoon salt
3 cups sugar	1¼ cups milk
5 large eggs	4 tablespoons grated bittersweet chocolate
3 cups unbleached all-purpose flour	1 teaspoon vanilla extract

1. Preheat the oven to 325°F. Lightly grease and flour a
9-inch bundt cake pan.

2. In a large bowl, cream the butter, shortening, and sugar
together until light and fluffy. Add the eggs, one at a time, beating well after each addition.

3. In another bowl, sift together the flour, cocoa, baking powder, and salt. Add the dry ingredients to the butter mixture,
alternating in batches with the milk and mixing well after each
addition. Mix in the grated chocolate and vanilla.

4. Pour the batter into the prepared pan and bake for
1½ hours, or until set, when a toothpick inserted in the cake
comes out clean. Cool the cake on a wire rack.

MAKES ONE 9-INCH BUNDT CAKE

DOUBLE CHOCOLATE BROWNIES

*These brownies created by our Shaker baker, George Covey,
truly exemplify the Shakers' quest for creating an earthly heaven.
So bring on the milk . . . by the gallons, because these are going
to knock your socks off!*

½ cup (1 stick) unsalted
butter
1 cup plus 2 tablespoons
sugar
3 tablespoons water
3 cups semisweet
chocolate chips, divided
3 large eggs, beaten

½ teaspoon vanilla extract
1 cup plus 2 tablespoons
unbleached all-purpose
flour
½ teaspoon salt
¼ teaspoon baking soda
¾ cup small walnut pieces

1. Preheat the oven to 350°F. Lightly grease a 13- by 9- by
2-inch baking pan.

2. Combine the butter, sugar, and water in a large saucepan,
and bring to a boil over medium heat. Remove the pan from the
heat. Add 1½ cups chocolate chips and stir until melted. Stir in
the beaten eggs and vanilla.

3. In a bowl, combine the flour, salt, baking soda, walnuts,
and the remaining 1½ cups chocolate chips. Add to the saucepan
and mix well. Pour the batter into the prepared pan and spread
the batter evenly. Bake for 25 minutes, or until a toothpick inserted in the brownies comes out clean. Cool the brownies on a
wire rack, then cut into squares.

MAKES APPROXIMATELY 2 DOZEN

BAKED INDIAN PUDDING WITH BOILED CIDER WALNUT ICE CREAM

The Shakers varied the recipe in several ways, from how it was sweetened—either sugar, molasses, or maple syrup—to what should accompany it—cream, hard sauce, or ice cream.

I was tempted to include a dozen different recipes for this pudding but I've managed to narrow it down to this one. The Shakers suggest serving this recipe with Boiled Cider Walnut Ice Cream (page 150), but warm cream or Old-Fashioned Hard Sauce (opposite) are also quite appealing.

5 cups milk, divided
5 tablespoons unsalted butter
1 cup stone-ground yellow cornmeal (see Sources)
2 large eggs, beaten
⅓ cup maple syrup, preferably dark amber or grade B

⅓ cup molasses
2 tablespoons sugar
½ teaspoon salt
½ teaspoon ground cinnamon
¼ teaspoon ground ginger
⅛ teaspoon ground allspice

1. Preheat the oven to 325°F. Lightly butter a 2-quart baking dish.

2. In a large saucepan, heat 4 cups milk and the butter to a boil, stirring until the butter melts. Add the cornmeal and stir vigorously until the mixture is smooth and thick, about 4 to 5 minutes. Remove from the heat and allow to cool for 10 minutes. Add the eggs, maple syrup, molasses, sugar, salt, cinnamon, ginger, and allspice, and mix well.

3. Pour into the prepared dish and bake for 1 hour. Pour the remaining cup of cold milk over the hot pudding and bake for an additional 1 to 1½ hours. Serve the pudding hot.

SERVES APPROXIMATELY 8

SISTER EDITH'S GREAT-GRANDMOTHER'S INDIAN PUDDING

Edith M. Green (1879–1951) came to live with the Canterbury Shakers at the age of sixteen. In my collection of Shaker ephemera I have what's believed to be Sister Edith's first cook's journal. The handwritten booklet is titled "Edith Green, Canterbury North Family, 1896" and contains numerous recipes for sweets: Gingered Suet Pudding, Baked Apple Dumplings, Potato Chocolate Cake, and this Indian Pudding recipe passed down from her great-grandmother.

Stir one cup of I. meal into 1 qt. of milk. Let boil a few minutes and add one cup of molasses, 1 teaspoon salt, 1 teaspoon cinnamon and 10 large sweet apples, sliced. Stir in a qt. of cold milk and bake in a slow oven 5 hours. Serve with sweetened cream or hard sauce.

OLD-FASHIONED HARD SAUCE

Many say that old-fashioned steamed puddings are not complete without hard sauce. Who am I to argue? Here's our recipe for good basic hard sauce.

½ cup (1 stick) unsalted butter
1½ cups confectioners' sugar

Pinch of salt
1 teaspoon vanilla extract

In a small mixing bowl, cream the butter, sugar, and salt until light and fluffy. Add the vanilla and mix well. Refrigerate, tightly covered, until needed, up to 5 days.

MAKES APPROXIMATELY 1 CUP

STEAMED CHOCOLATE PUDDING

The recipe for this classic New England dessert comes directly from the Village's archives. Try it with Old-Fashioned Hard Sauce (page 133) or with Bittersweet Chocolate Sauce (page 167) and whipped cream for a decadent finale.

¾ cup sugar
⅓ cup unsalted butter
2 large eggs
1 teaspoon baking powder
1¼ cups unbleached all-
    purpose flour

1 tablespoon Dutch cocoa
    powder
½ teaspoon salt
¾ cup milk
½ teaspoon vanilla extract

1. In a large bowl, cream the sugar and butter, then add the eggs, one at a time, scraping down the sides of the bowl.

2. Sift the baking powder, flour, cocoa, and salt together, and add alternately to the creamed mixture with the milk. Add the vanilla.

3. Heat 1 inch of water in a large pot with a lid to a simmer over medium heat. Grease a 1-pound coffee can. Pour the batter into the prepared coffee can, cover tightly with aluminum foil, and steam in the pot, covered, for 1 hour.

4. Remove the can from the pot and allow to cool for 10 minutes. Remove the pudding from the can, slice, and serve warm with the desired topping.

SERVES 4 TO 6

BUTTERSCOTCH PECAN BARS

Another favorite treat of museum visitors created by our baker, George Covey, these are best when served within a few hours after baking and better still when served warm with a scoop of Old-Fashioned Vanilla Bean Ice Cream (page 145) and topped with Caramel Sauce (page 168) and whipped cream. Not for the calorie-conscious.

½ cup (1 stick) unsalted butter
1 cup plus 2 tablespoons sugar
3 tablespoons water
3 cups butterscotch chips, divided
3 large eggs, beaten

½ teaspoon vanilla extract
1 cup plus 2 tablespoons unbleached all-purpose flour
½ teaspoon salt
¼ teaspoon baking soda
¾ cup small pecan pieces

1. Preheat the oven to 350°F. Lightly grease a 13- by 9- by 2-inch baking pan.

2. Combine the butter, sugar, and water in a large saucepan, and heat to a boil over medium heat. Remove the pan from the head. Add 1½ cups butterscotch chips and stir until melted. Stir in the beaten eggs and vanilla.

3. In a large bowl, combine the flour, salt, baking soda, pecans, and the remaining 1½ cups butterscotch chips. Add to the saucepan and mix well. Pour the batter into the prepared pan and spread the batter evenly. Bake for 25 minutes, or until a toothpick inserted in the bars comes out clean. Cool the bars on a wire rack and cut into squares. Top as desired.

MAKES APPROXIMATELY 2 DOZEN

BOILED CIDER PIE

This recipe is traditionally a double-crusted pie. I lightened it up a bit by eliminating the top crust. The boiled cider makes for a delicate custard with a very interesting texture and unique taste, needing nothing more than a dollop of Cinnamon-Flavored Whipped Cream (page 136).

4 large eggs	**1½ cups milk**
⅓ cup sugar	**1 teaspoon vanilla extract**
½ teaspoon salt	**1 unbaked 9-inch**
1 cup boiled cider (see	**deep-dish piecrust**
Sources)	**(page 168)**

1. Preheat the oven to 400°F.

2. In a large bowl, combine the eggs, sugar, and salt, and mix until pale yellow. Stir in the boiled cider, milk, and vanilla, and mix well. Pour into the prepared pie dish.

3. Bake for 10 minutes, then reduce the oven temperature to 350°F. and bake for 30 minutes, or until set, when a toothpick inserted in the center of the pie comes out clean. Cool the pie on a wire rack, then refrigerate, covered. Serve the pie cool with a dollop of Cinnamon-Flavored Whipped Cream, if desired.

MAKES ONE 9-INCH DEEP-DISH PIE

CINNAMON-FLAVORED
WHIPPED CREAM

1 tablespoon sugar	**1 cup heavy cream**
¼ teaspoon ground	
cinnamon	

In a cold bowl, combine the sugar and cinnamon. Slowly whisk in a little cream to dissolve the cinnamon. Add the remaining cream, and whip by hand or with a blender on medium speed until it reaches the desired stiffness.

MAKES APPROXIMATELY 2 CUPS

COCONUT CUSTARD PIE

For coconut lovers only, this is a simple variation on the traditional custard pie using coconut milk in the custard and flaked coconut in the crust.

CRUST

1 cup unbleached
   all-purpose flour
2 tablespoons
   unsweetened shredded
   coconut
¼ teaspoon salt

1 tablespoon sugar
3 tablespoons chilled lard
   or vegetable shortening
3 tablespoons chilled
   unsalted butter
¼ cup cold heavy cream

FILLING

4 large eggs
⅔ cup sugar
½ teaspoon salt

1½ cups coconut milk
1 cup light cream
1 teaspoon vanilla extract

1. Preheat the oven to 425°F.

TO MAKE THE CRUST

2. In a large bowl or the bowl of a food processor, combine the flour, coconut, salt, and sugar. Cut the lard and butter into the flour until it resembles coarse meal. Add the cream gradually and mix until the dough comes together. Knead the dough until smooth and refrigerate, well wrapped, for at least 1 hour.

3. Roll out the pie dough on a lightly floured surface, no more than ¼ inch thick, and line a 9-inch deep-dish pie pan. Refrigerate, covered, until needed.

TO MAKE THE FILLING

4. In a mixing bowl, combine the eggs, sugar, and salt, and mix until blended. Stir in the coconut milk, cream, and vanilla, and pour the filling into the prepared pie dish.

5. Bake for 10 minutes, then reduce the oven to 350°F. and bake for 30 minutes, or until set, when a toothpick inserted in the center of the pie comes out clean. Cool the pie on a wire rack, then refrigerate, covered, for at least an hour.

MAKES ONE 9-INCH DEEP-DISH PIE

SISTER ETHEL'S DEEP-DISH CUSTARD PIE

Custard pie was a favorite of the Shakers. Sister Ethel recalls making hundreds of these pies during her lifetime working in the village's bakery, built in 1820.

Deep-dish custard pie was her favorite and she dictated her recipe to me. When she finished, I asked her, "Is that everything?" She quickly replied, "I almost forgot the most important ingredients, a little love and devotion. That's what really makes it taste so good."

4 large eggs	**1 teaspoon vanilla extract**
⅔ cup sugar	**¼ teaspoon grated nutmeg**
½ teaspoon salt	**1 unbaked 9-inch**
1¼ cups milk	**deep-dish piecrust**
1¼ cups light cream	**(page 168)**

1. Preheat the oven to 425°F.

2. In a large bowl, combine the eggs, sugar, and salt, and mix until blended. Stir in the milk, cream, vanilla, and nutmeg, and pour into the prepared pie dish.

3. Bake for 10 minutes, then reduce the oven to 350°F. and bake for 30 more minutes, or until set, when a toothpick inserted in the center of the pie comes out clean. Cool the pie on a wire rack, then refrigerate for at least 1 hour before serving.

MAKES ONE 9-INCH DEEP-DISH PIE

RHUBARB CUSTARD
MERINGUE PIE

The original Shaker recipe calls for placing chopped rhubarb in the bottom of a pie pan, pouring the custard over, and baking. In my version of this spring treat, I blend stewed rhubarb into the custard, giving the pie a creamy rhubarb flavor throughout.

2 cups small diced rhubarb, washed	**½ cup sugar** **¼ cup water**
1½ cups heavy cream **4 extra-large eggs, beaten** **1 teaspoon vanilla extract**	**1 to 2 tablespoons sugar (optional)**
1 unbaked 10-inch deep-dish piecrust (page 170)	
4 extra-large egg whites	**⅔ cup extra-fine sugar**

TO MAKE THE RHUBARB PUREE

1. Combine the rhubarb, sugar, and water in a heavy saucepan. Heat to a boil over medium heat and cook, stirring often, until it becomes a smooth puree, about 10 minutes.

TO MAKE THE CUSTARD

2. Preheat the oven to 375°F.

3. In a large bowl combine the cream, eggs, and vanilla. Stir in the rhubarb puree. Add sugar to taste if necessary. Pour the mixture into the prepared pie pan. Bake 30 minutes or until the custard is set, when a toothpick inserted comes out clean.

TO MAKE THE MERINGUE

4. Reduce the oven temperature to 300°F.

5. In a very clean bowl, beat the egg whites until soft peaks start to form. As you continue to beat, slowly add the sugar, and continue to beat until stiff peaks are formed.

6. Spoon the meringue onto the pie. With a metal cake spatula, spread the meringue evenly over the top of the pie. Return the pie to the oven for 15 to 20 minutes, or until the meringue is lightly browned. Serve the pie at room temperature or chilled.

ROSE WATER–APPLE PIE

The Shakers raised dozens of different varieties of apples, but for apple pie the Sisters always recommended Granny Smiths. In the early days the only flavorings the Shakers had were homemade lemon, orange, and rose waters. This pie, shared with us by Eldress Bertha, uses rose water to give the pie a unique fragrance. Eldress Bertha made this pie for friends and company almost up until the day she passed away at the age of ninety-four. We still make rose water–apple pie every fall; apple-picking time wouldn't be the same without it.

Double recipe Old-Fashioned Lard Piecrust (page 168)
6 large Granny Smith apples
¼ to ½ cup sugar (see Note)
3 tablespoons unbleached all-purpose flour

1 teaspoon rose water (see Sources)
1 large egg, beaten
Old-Fashioned Vanilla Bean Ice Cream (page 145) or extra-sharp Vermont Cheddar cheese (optional)

1. Preheat the oven to 375°F.

2. On a lightly floured surface, roll out half of the pie dough into a 12-inch circle, ¼ inch thick. Line a 9-inch deep-dish pie pan with the dough. Roll out the remaining piece of dough on a lightly floured surface into a 13-inch circle, ¼ inch thick, to make the top crust and set aside.

3. Peel, core, and cut each apple into 8 equal wedges. In a large bowl, toss the apples with the sugar and flour until well coated. Pile the apples into the prepared pie pan, mounding them higher in the center. Sprinkle the rose water evenly over the apples.

4. With a pastry brush, brush the edges of the pie shell with the beaten egg, drape the top crust over the pie, and crimp the edges to seal the 2 crusts together. Brush the top crust with water and sprinkle lightly with additional sugar. Cut 4 to 6 slits in the top crust to allow steam to escape during baking. Place the pie on a baking sheet and bake on the lowest shelf of the oven for 1 hour.

5. Serve the pie warm or at room temperature with Old-Fashioned Vanilla Bean Ice Cream or a wedge of extra-sharp Vermont Cheddar cheese.

MAKES ONE 9-INCH DEEP-DISH PIE

NOTE: The amount of sugar used depends upon the tartness of the apples and your own personal taste.

CHOCOLATE WALNUT PIE

The Canterbury Shakers used to grow walnut trees, which, in typical Shaker fashion, they used for everything from their sturdy wood for cabinets to their flavorful nuts.

This pie is best served at room temperature with Bittersweet Chocolate Sauce (page 167) and whipped cream or, for the ultimate indulgence, a scoop of Wild Turkey Ice Cream (variation on page 145).

½ cup dark corn syrup
¼ cup (½ stick) unsalted
    butter
¼ cup cocoa powder
¼ cup plus 2 tablespoons
    sugar
¼ teaspoon salt

2 large eggs, lightly beaten
1 teaspoon vanilla extract
2 cups small walnut pieces
1 unbaked 9-inch
    deep-dish piecrust
    (page 168)

1. Preheat the oven to 375°F.

2. In a small saucepan, heat the corn syrup and butter over low heat until the butter is melted.

3. In a large bowl, sift together the cocoa powder, sugar, and salt. Stir in the eggs and vanilla, blending until the batter is smooth. Stir in the corn syrup mixture and nuts. Pour the batter into the unbaked crust.

4. Bake the pie for 30 minutes, or until a toothpick inserted in the center comes out clean. Cool the pie on a wire rack.

MAKES ONE 9-INCH DEEP-DISH PIE

SHAKER MINCE MEAT Sister Leona Merrill Rowell came to live with the Canterbury Shakers at age eight in 1913. She apprenticed under Sisters Ida Crook and Helena Sarle in the bake room where she learned how to make wonderful pies and breads. She left the Shaker society in 1935 but remained very close with the Sisters. I had the pleasure of meeting Leona in the summer of 1988 and struck up a wonderful friendship. On her visits to the Village she'd always poke her head in the kitchen to see what was cooking. If by chance we were making pies or bread, she'd jump right in and show us how it was supposed to be done. We learned a lot from her as we did from all of the Sisters. To this day she made the best apple pie I've ever had in my life.

Leona and I really weren't quite sure how old this recipe for Shaker mincemeat is. I do know that it's the recipe she used back in the late 1920s and was handed down to her by an elder Sister.

Leona passed away in the winter of 1992. We all miss her, the kitchen staff especially, for her deep-dish apple pies.

> 5 lbs. neck meat, cooked and ground
> 4 quarts sour apple, ground
> 1 lb. ground suet
> 1 pt. boiled cider
> 2 lbs. brown sugar
> 1 or more tumblers of jelly (any kind)
> grated rind and juice of 2 lemons
> 2 nutmegs, grated
> 2 tblsp. cinnamon
> 1 tblsp. cloves
> 2 lbs. raisins
> 1 pot of coffee

—Combine everything and cook all afternoon.

SHAKER SOUR CREAM PIE

I re-created this recipe from a conversation with Sister Ethel. She basically described this unique pie as a custard pie for which you substitute sour cream for the milk and add raisins.

1 unbaked 10-inch
   deep-dish piecrust
   (page 170)
1 cup raisins
3 extra-large egg yolks
1 extra-large egg
2 cups sour cream

½ cup maple syrup,
   preferably dark amber
   or grade B
1 teaspoon ground
   cinnamon
1 teaspoon vanilla extract
1 tablespoon all-purpose
   flour

1. Preheat the oven to 375°F.

2. In the bottom of the unbaked pie crust, evenly distribute the raisins.

3. In a bowl or blender combine the egg yolks, egg, sour cream, maple syrup, cinnamon, vanilla, and flour. Mix just until blended. Pour the mixture into the prepared pie pan.

4. Bake 30 minutes or until set, when a toothpick inserted comes out clean. Cool to room temperature, then refrigerate up to 2 days. This pie is best eaten the day it is made.

MAKES ONE 10-INCH DEEP-DISH PIE

MAPLE BUTTERNUT PIE

Sweet butternut meats require a great deal of patience to harvest because their shells are extremely hard to crack. Sister Ethel used to joke about how the kitchen Sisters used to have to "whack the nuts with a great big mallet, sometimes two or three times before the shells would crack." If you're fortunate enough to have butternut trees on your property and a lot of time to kill, or know of a good butternut source, this pie is for you.

Today these nuts are not so readily available on a commercial basis, basically because of the time required to shell them. Pecans or walnuts both work equally well as a substitute in this recipe.

1 unbaked 10-inch deep-
    dish piecrust
    (page 170)
2½ cups chopped sweet
    butternut meats or
    2 cups pecan halves
    (see Sources)
4 extra-large eggs, beaten

1 cup maple syrup,
    preferably dark amber
    or grade B
1 tablespoon cider vinegar
1 teaspoon vanilla extract
2 tablespoons melted
    unsalted butter
Old-Fashioned Vanilla
    Bean Ice Cream
    (page 145)

1. Preheat the oven to 375°F.

2. In the bottom of the unbaked pie crust, evenly distribute the butternut meats.

3. In a mixing bowl combine the eggs, maple syrup, cider vinegar, and vanilla and mix until blended. Stir in the melted butter. Pour the mixture into the prepared pie pan.

4. Bake 30 minutes or until the pie is set, firm to the touch. Serve at room temperature with the ice cream.

MAKES ONE 10-INCH DEEP-DISH PIE

OLD-FASHIONED VANILLA BEAN ICE CREAM

This is the basic recipe, the foundation if you will, on which all of my ice cream creations are built. Rich, creamy, and completely delicious.

2 cups milk	**1 vanilla bean**
2 cups heavy cream	**12 large egg yolks**
1 cup sugar, divided	

1. In a large heavy saucepan, combine the milk, cream, and half of the sugar. Cut the vanilla bean in half lengthwise and scrape the seeds into the saucepan, then add the bean pod itself.

2. Heat to just below the boiling point over medium heat, stirring occasionally. Remove the saucepan from the heat. Allow to cool for 30 minutes, stirring occasionally.

3. In a large metal bowl, combine the egg yolks and remaining sugar and beat until pale yellow. Slowly whisk the scalded liquid into the egg yolk mixture.

4. Place the metal bowl over a double boiler on low heat. Cook, stirring constantly, until the mixture thickens and coats the back of a spoon, approximately 5 to 7 minutes. Strain the mixture, removing the bean pod, and cool completely, uncovered. (This mixture can be refrigerated overnight, covered, before freezing.)

5. Freeze in an ice cream maker according to the manufacturer's directions.

MAKES APPROXIMATELY 1½ QUARTS

VARIATION

For Wild Turkey Ice Cream: In a large heavy saucepan, pour 1 cup Wild Turkey liquor. With a long match carefully ignite the liquor and allow the alcohol to burn off, until the flame extinguishes. Reduce the liquor over medium-low heat until reduced to about ½ cup. Add to the ice cream during step 5.

ICE CREAM The Canterbury Shakers raised pure-bred, registered Guernsey, a breed of cattle noted for high milk production and high butterfat content in the milk, two important criteria in making cheese, butter, and ice cream. Their cattle, especially two cows named Lilly Bell and Canterbury Bell, won several awards and, when auctioned off in 1920, brought the highest price ever paid in New Hampshire.

Homemade ice cream and sherbet held a special place in the heart of Eldress Bertha Lindsay. She often spoke to me of her grandfather, Grandpa Lindsay, as one of the inventors of the original White Mountain Ice Cream Freezer in the 1850s. We have three original White Mountain freezers in Canterbury Shaker Village's collection today, with their venerable history.

Christmas of 1926 proved to be a very special day for the Village's kitchen Sisters, for Brother Irving Greenwood purchased them a used electric Kitchen Aid mixer. In January of the new year, Brother Irving motorized one of the White Mountain ice cream freezers, using the Kitchen Aid mixer as the power source, Shaker ingenuity at its finest. No more cranking ice cream by hand. An unidentified kitchen Sister composed this poem to commemorate that very special day:

When we cooks now play the Kitchen Aid
All the grinders, sieves, and fancy beaters
Have been relegated to the shelf,
For we simply touch a little lever,
And the ice cream will make itself.

Today, I still continue to make our ice cream from scratch, using a motorized White Mountain Freezer that still relies on rock salt and lots and lots of crushed ice. Our flavors are a blend of traditional and contemporary. Whenever I created a new flavor I would always bring a sample to the Sisters, seeking their approval. I can't tell what intrigued the Sisters more, the names of the creations or the actual tasting!!!

NATIVE WILD BLUEBERRY LAVENDER ICE CREAM

In case it's not obvious that blueberries and lavender are one of my favorite combinations, here's yet another recipe that highlights these two great tastes in one cool summer treat!

2 cups milk	**1 vanilla bean**
2 cups heavy cream	**12 large egg yolks**
1 cup sugar, divided	**1 pint wild blueberries,**
4 fresh lavender sprigs,	**the smaller the better,**
washed	**washed and picked over**

1. In a large heavy saucepan, combine the milk, cream, half of the sugar, and the lavender sprigs. Cut the vanilla bean in half lengthwise and scrape the seeds into the saucepan, then add the bean pod itself.

2. Heat to just below the boiling point over medium heat, stirring occasionally. Remove from the heat.

3. In a large metal bowl, combine the egg yolks and the remaining sugar and beat until pale yellow. Slowly whisk the scalded liquid into the egg yolk mixture, remove the lavender sprigs and the vanilla bean, and discard.

4. Place the metal bowl over a double boiler on low heat. Cook, stirring constantly, until the mixture thickens and coats the back of a spoon, approximately 5 to 7 minutes. Strain the mixture, removing the bean pod, and cool completely, uncovered. (This mixture can be refrigerated overnight, covered, before freezing.)

5. Freeze in an ice cream maker according to the manufacturer's directions. When the ice cream is almost done but still soft, fold in the blueberries and then continue to freeze the ice cream.

MAKES APPROXIMATELY 1 QUART

REAL CHOCOLATE MINT ICE CREAM

You won't find any chocolate chips in this ice cream. The wonderful old-fashioned chocolate peppermint patty taste comes from the herb, chocolate mint. If chocolate mint is unavailable, you could substitute spearmint or peppermint, which will result in fresh minty ice cream, and add a cup or so of the highest quality chocolate chips you can find.

1 cup fresh chocolate mint leaves, washed
2 cups milk
2 cups heavy cream
1 cup sugar, divided
1 vanilla bean
12 large egg yolks

1. In a large heavy saucepan, combine the mint, milk, cream, and half of the sugar. Cut the vanilla bean in half lengthwise and scrape the seeds into the saucepan, then add the bean pod itself.

2. Heat to just below the boiling point over medium heat, stirring occasionally. Remove the saucepan from the heat. Allow to cool for 30 minutes, stirring occasionally.

3. In a large metal bowl, combine the egg yolks and the remaining sugar and beat until pale yellow. Slowly whisk the scalded liquid into the egg mixture. Strain out the mint leaves and discard.

4. Place the metal bowl over a double boiler on low heat. Cook, stirring constantly, until the mixture thickens and coats the back of a spoon, approximately 5 to 7 minutes. Strain the mixture, removing the bean pod, and cool completely, uncovered. (This mixture can be refrigerated overnight, covered, before freezing.)

5. Freeze in an ice cream maker according to the manufacturer's directions.

MAKES APPROXIMATELY 1½ QUARTS

VARIATION

For Minted Chocolate Chip Ice Cream: Substitute fresh spearmint leaves for the chocolate mint leaves. When the ice cream is almost frozen but still soft, add a cup or so of the best quality bittersweet chocolate chips you can find, then continue to freeze the ice cream.

MINTED CHOCOLATE CHIP ICE CREAM SANDWICHES

I think we all have fond memories from our childhoods about savoring ice cream sandwiches on a hot summers' day. With a little imagination, ice cream sandwiches can be lifted to new heights.

Minted Chocolate Chip Ice Cream (variation on page 148)

1 cup (2 sticks) unsalted butter	1 teaspoon vanilla extract
½ cup sugar	2¾ cups cake flour
1 large egg	⅔ cup cocoa powder
	¼ teaspoon salt

1. Prepare the Minted Chocolate Chip Ice Cream.

TO MAKE THE CHOCOLATE WAFERS

2. Preheat the oven to 375°F.

3. In a large bowl, cream the butter and sugar until smooth. Add the egg and vanilla and mix well.

4. In a large bowl, sift together the flour, cocoa powder, and salt, and mix into the butter mixture until the dough resembles cookie dough. Refrigerate the dough for 1 hour.

5. Roll out the dough on a lightly floured surface ¼ inch thick. With a floured 3½-inch-round cutter, cut out as many circles as possible. Excess dough can be rerolled once to cut additional circles (for a total of 24). Transfer the dough rounds to a parchment paper–lined baking sheet using a spatula. Prick each wafer several times with a fork. Bake for 12 to 15 minutes. Transfer to a wire rack and cool.

TO MAKE THE ICE CREAM SANDWICHES

6. Place a scoop of freshly made ice cream on a wafer, top with another wafer, and gently press to evenly distribute the ice cream filling. Wrap the sandwiches in plastic wrap and freeze. Repeat this process until all of the wafers are used. Allow the sandwiches to freeze a minimum of 2 hours before serving.

MAKES 12 SANDWICHES

BOILED CIDER WALNUT
ICE CREAM

Boiled cider, like rose water, was a natural flavoring produced by the Shakers to take the place of vanilla. It was also used as a substitute for sugar in making cakes, pies, puddings, jellies, and ice creams.

The process for making boiled cider is similar to that of maple syrup. The Shakers would start with fresh cider and slowly reduce it to an apple concentrate, about a quarter of its original volume.

George, the Village baker, and I still make boiled cider every fall. It's a long process but one we look forward to every year. You can purchase very good boiled cider from one of several reputable New England producers (see Sources).

2 cups milk	**12 large egg yolks**
2 cups heavy cream	**1 cup boiled cider, chilled**
1 cup sugar, divided	**1 cup small walnut pieces**

1. In a large heavy saucepan, combine the milk, cream, and half of the sugar. Heat to just below the boiling point over medium heat, stirring occasionally. Remove the saucepan from the heat. Allow to cool for 30 minutes, stirring often.

2. In a large metal bowl, combine the egg yolks and remaining sugar and beat until pale yellow. Slowly whisk the scalded liquid into the egg yolk mixture.

3. Place the metal bowl over a double boiler on low heat. Cook, stirring constantly, until the mixture thickens and coats the back of a spoon, approximately 5 to 7 minutes. Strain the mixture and cool completely, uncovered. (This mixture can be refrigerated overnight, covered, before freezing.)

4. Stir the boiled cider into the cold ice cream base. Freeze in an ice cream maker according to the manufacturer's directions. When the ice cream is almost done but still soft, add the walnut pieces, then continue to freeze the ice cream.

MAKES APPROXIMATELY 2 QUARTS

AGRICULTURE

Get the best and never keep a poor cow the second year. No man can afford to keep a cow that will not make 200 to 220 lbs. of butter or its equivalent in cheese every year.

THE SHAKER MANIFESTO   JULY 1879

LEMON–POPPY SEED–SOUR CREAM ICE CREAM

I'm very passionate about my ice cream creations. I stumbled upon this version one afternoon while playing in the kitchen. I was wondering what frozen sour cream would taste like. This may seem like a very strange concoction, but the sour cream makes an incredibly, sinfully rich ice cream and the poppy seeds add an interesting texture. In my opinion, it begs to accompany a dish of warm Wild Blueberry Cobbler (page 126).

2 pints sour cream　　　**2 teaspoons lemon zest**
1½ cups sugar　　　　　**Juice of 3 lemons**
2 tablespoons poppy seeds

　　1. In a large bowl or the bowl of a food processor, combine all of the ingredients. Stir or process until the ingredients are smoothly blended with no lumps.

　　2. Freeze in an ice cream maker according to the manufacturer's directions.

MAKES APPROXIMATELY 1 QUART

WARM GINGER PEACHES WITH WHITE CHOCOLATE ICE CREAM

2 tablespoons (¼ stick) unsalted butter
¼ cup light brown sugar
1 teaspoon honey
¼ teaspoon minced fresh peeled gingerroot
½ teaspoon orange zest
1 tablespoon fresh orange juice

2 medium peaches, washed, pitted, and thinly sliced
2 tablespoons Grand Marnier or other orange liqueur
4 scoops White Chocolate Ice Cream (page 154) or vanilla ice cream

1. In a large skillet, melt the butter, brown sugar, and honey over low heat, stirring occasionally.

2. Add the gingerroot, orange zest, orange juice, and peaches, and sauté for 1 to 2 minutes over medium heat. Remove the skillet from the heat, add the liqueur, carefully flambé with a long match, and return the pan to low heat. Allow the flame to burn out. Simmer the peaches until they are soft and the sauce is the consistency of a light syrup.

3. Place a scoop of White Chocolate Ice Cream in 4 serving bowls and evenly distribute the peaches and syrup over the ice cream. Serve immediately.

SERVES 4

WARM BANANA PECAN COMPOTE OVER VANILLA BEAN ICE CREAM AND GRIDDLED BANANA BREAD

Fresh slices of banana are simmered in butter, brown sugar, and spices, then poured over ice cream and a slice of griddled banana bread.

2 tablespoons (¼ stick) unsalted butter
¼ cup light brown sugar
1 teaspoon honey
Pinch of ground cinnamon
Pinch of nutmeg
2 medium bananas, peeled and sliced ¼ inch thick

¼ cup small pecan pieces
4 slices of Banana Nut Bread (page 45), cut ½ inch thick
Butter for spreading
2 tablespoons dark rum
4 scoops Old-Fashioned Vanilla Bean Ice Cream (page 145)

1. In a large skillet, melt the butter, brown sugar, and honey over low heat, stirring occasionally.

2. Stir in the cinnamon and nutmeg. Add the sliced bananas and pecan pieces, and sauté, stirring gently, for 1 to 2 minutes over medium heat.

3. Meanwhile, lightly butter the slices of banana bread on both sides. Cook on a griddle or in a frying pan (350°F. on an electric griddle) over medium heat until golden brown on both sides, approximately 1 minute per side.

4. Remove the skillet with the bananas from the heat, add the rum, carefully flambé with a long match, and return the pan to low heat. Allow the flame to burn out. Simmer the bananas until they are soft and the sauce is the consistency of a light syrup.

5. Place a slice of warm griddled banana bread on each serving dish, top with a scoop of Old-Fashioned Vanilla Bean Ice Cream, and evenly distribute the warm bananas and syrup over the ice cream. Serve immediately.

SERVES 4

WHITE CHOCOLATE ICE CREAM

Sister Ethel was my biggest fan when it came to my ice cream "concoctions." Her favorite flavors were strawberry and chocolate. I decided to surprise her one hot summer afternoon with a big bowl of White Chocolate Ice Cream, and surprise her I did.

2 cups milk	½ pound white chocolate,
2 cups heavy cream	coarsely chopped
¾ cup sugar, divided	1 teaspoon vanilla extract
8 large egg yolks	

1. In a large heavy saucepan, combine the milk, cream, and half of the sugar. Heat to just below the boiling point over medium heat. Remove the saucepan from the heat and allow to cool for 30 minutes, stirring occasionally.

2. In a large metal bowl, combine the egg yolks and remaining sugar and beat until pale yellow. Slowly whisk the scalded milk mixture into the egg mixture.

3. Place the metal bowl over a double boiler on low heat. Cook, stirring constantly, until the mixture thickens and coats the back of a spoon, approximately 5 to 7 minutes. Remove the bowl from the double boiler, add the chocolate and vanilla, and stir until the chocolate is melted. Strain the mixture and cool completely, uncovered. (This mixture can be refrigerated overnight, covered, before freezing.)

4. Freeze in an ice cream maker according to the manufacturer's directions.

MAKES APPROXIMATELY 1½ QUARTS

GINGER HONEY SAUCE

The recipe for this sauce was given to me by Brian Hennington, the first chef I trained under some fourteen years ago. This is just incredible over White Chocolate Ice Cream (page 154) with Griddled Banana Bread (page 153, step 3) and a dollop of whipped cream.

1 cup honey
1 cup (2 sticks) unsalted
  butter
1 cup light brown sugar

1 to 2 tablespoons
  julienned peeled
  gingerroot

1. In a large heavy saucepan, combine the honey, butter, and brown sugar, and heat over medium-low heat to a boil, stirring often. Stir in the julienned gingerroot and continue to cook, stirring, for 1 minute.

2. Serve warm over ice cream (see Note) and banana bread, if desired, with whipped cream.

SERVES 8

NOTE: The sauce may be made ahead of time and gently reheated when needed. Keep in the refrigerator, covered, up to 5 days.

FRESH BERRY SYRUP

This light, concentrated berry syrup goes well with breakfast entrées as well as desserts. I prefer to make this syrup with fresh berries; however, frozen will work almost as well.

2 pints fresh raspberries or
  berries of choice,
  washed and picked over

½ cup water
¾ cup sugar, or more as
  needed

1. In a saucepan, combine the berries, water, and ¾ cup sugar to start with, and mash with a spoon. Heat the mixture to a boil over medium heat, stirring frequently, then lower the heat and simmer for approximately 10 minutes.

2. Adjust the sweetness to taste and strain the mixture. Cool completely. Refrigerate, covered, until needed, up to 5 days.

MAKES APPROXIMATELY 1½ CUPS

VISIT TO AND OBSERVATIONS UPON A FORTY-ACRE FRUIT FARM

[Our very observing and talented brother, Daniel Fraser, has been taking notes and he writes us some very worthy considerations.]

First. Raspberries, (black and red) the rows of which are seven feet apart, and about three feet apart in the rows. A leading feature in their culture is, that the canes when about two feet six inches high are pinched. The results are, side shoots are thrown out, increasing the bearing wood, and improving the fruit. The canes being low, winter better, and are not so liable as long canes are to be lashed about with the winds. Only two canes are allowed to a hill.

A plantation when the old canes are removed has a fine appearance; each cane with its branches is like a little tree, several acres together have quite a pleasing effect. When the sides of the shoots get too long they are cut to the right length.

The old canes are removed top a heap, not to be burnt, but to decompose, and then applied to young plantations. Such a heap, composed of earth and sods, and brush, and on the top a layer of wood ashes, and a layer of lime, and exposed to gentle rains so as to saturate the heap, becomes a chemical laboratory, wherein the nitrogen of the atmosphere is detached from the air, forming the nitrate of potash, the most valuable of all manurial salts.

Berry culture can never be a permanent success without a system of rotation. The black raspberry may be renewed every six years, the red, eight; the blackberry, every ten years; strawberries, every two years; if grown in hills and well cared for, they will run well for several years.

One of the best dressings for fruits of all kinds is wood ashes, two bushels; lime, two bushels; salt, two bushels; in all six bushels per acre. If the land is rich in potash and lime, salt and plaster will be good.

On laying out a raspberry plantation, plant so as to be able to cultivate both ways, and every four rows leave narrow roads to facilitate the removal of fruit and brush.

On this berry farm, the strawberries are renewed every two years; planted in the spring one foot apart in the rows. Spaces are left so that the fruit can be picked without stepping on the plants, and to admit of cultivation. After the first fruit crop is gathered the cultivator is run through the spaces, and then the whole bed is harrowed, leaving the land loose and smooth for the runners to root in, thus furnishing plants for new plantations. Seventy bushels of strawberries were picked on this place one day. Of raspberries, in the fall of the season, a greater number of bushels is daily shipped.

CONTINUED

Berries in some degree create their own market, the fruit is mostly sold within twenty miles of the place. (Berlin, Rens. Co., N.Y.) Small fruits enter increasingly into the diet of the people, and inasmuch as they supersede the use of butter and meat in warm weather, all the better. Butter is hard on the liver, and yields but little support to the muscular and nervous tissues.

In addition to the great quantities of fresh fruits consumed, to a considerable extent they are also preserved. The single article of red raspberry jam consumed within fifteen miles of Boston amounts annually (according to the New England Grocer) to five hundred tons. The dried fruit is bought by the manufacturers at eighty-four cents a pound.

The blackberry succeeds the red raspberry, and connects with early apples and pears. The Wachusett blackberry in this locality completes the list of fruits. It embodies more good qualities than any other blackberry we know of, it bears abundantly, berries of good size, and of good quality. The canes are remarkably free from thorns, and being early, the fruit has brought even in panic times in the Boston market, thirty-three cents a quart.

The Wachusett was presented to the public by the Shakers at Shirley, Mass., by Leander Persons.

BASICS

STOCKS

Stocks are really the foundation upon which great soups and sauces are built. Although very time consuming to prepare, there is no substitute for homemade stocks. Canned broths may be used in the recipes throughout the book; however, I must warn you that the results will not be quite the same.

The process of making stocks exemplifies the kitchen philosophy of the Shakers. You use leftover parts of meat and ingredients and create a new, delicious, and versatile product.

I recommend making the stocks in larger batches and freezing the unused portion in one-quart containers to be used at a later date. The stock should keep one month in the freezer.

CHICKEN STOCK

**6 pounds chicken bones
and wings, mixed**
2½ quarts cold water
**2 large onions, peeled
and diced**
**2 large carrots, peeled
and diced**

**2 celery stalks, washed
and diced**
2 bay leaves
**5 sprigs fresh parsley,
washed**

1. Rinse the chicken bones and wings under cold water. In a large soup pot, combine the bones and wings with the water, and heat to a boil. Simmer over medium-low heat for 2 hours.

2. Add the onions, carrots, celery, bay leaves, and parsley, and simmer for another 2 hours. Skim the stock occasionally as it cooks.

3. Strain the stock and cool quickly. Refrigerate the stock, covered, until needed. Plan to use within 2 days or freeze.

MAKES APPROXIMATELY 1½ QUARTS

BEEF STOCK

6 pounds meaty beef and
   veal bones, mixed
3 quarts cold water
2 large onions, peeled and
   diced
2 carrots, peeled and diced

2 celery stalks, washed and
   diced
2 large tomatoes, chopped
2 cups red wine or water
2 bay leaves

1. Preheat the oven to 400°F.

2. Rinse the bones under cold water and drain well. Place the bones in a large roasting pan and roast for 1 hour, or until evenly browned.

3. Transfer the browned bones to a large soup pot, add the water, and bring to a boil over medium-high heat. Lower the heat to medium-low and simmer the stock for 5 hours. Skim the stock occasionally as it cooks.

4. Add the onions, carrots, celery, and tomatoes to the same roasting pan used for the bones. Roast the vegetables in the 400°F. oven 30 minutes, or until evenly browned.

5. Add the red wine or water to the roasting pan and deglaze the pan, scraping up all the bits on the bottom of the pan. Add everything to the soup pot. Stir in the bay leaves. Simmer the stock over medium-low heat for an additional 2 hours. Skim the stock occasionally as it cooks.

6. Strain the stock and cool quickly. Refrigerate the stock, covered, until needed. Plan to use within 2 days or freeze.

MAKES APPROXIMATELY 1½ QUARTS

FISH STOCK

5 pounds fish bones
2 quarts cold water
1 large onion, peeled and
diced
1 medium leek, sliced and
washed (including
greens)

2 carrots, peeled and diced
2 celery stalks, washed and
diced
2 bay leaves
5 sprigs fresh parsley

1. Rinse the bones under cold water.

2. In a large soup pot, combine the fish bones, water, onion, leek, carrots, celery, bay leaves, and parsley. Heat to a boil and simmer over medium-low heat for 30 to 45 minutes. Skim the stock occasionally as it cooks.

3. Strain the stock and cool quickly. Refrigerate the stock, covered, until needed. Use within 2 days or freeze.

MAKES APPROXIMATELY 2 QUARTS

PORK STOCK

6 pounds meaty pork
bones
2½ quarts plus 2 cups water
1 large onion, peeled and
diced
1 medium leek, sliced and
washed (whites only)

2 large carrots, peeled and
diced
2 celery stalks, washed and
diced
2 bay leaves
5 sprigs fresh parsley

1. Preheat the oven to 400°F.

2. Rinse the bones under cold water and drain well. Place the bones in a large roasting pan and roast for 1 hour, or until the bones are evenly browned.

3. Transfer the browned bones to a large soup pot, add the 2½ quarts water, and heat to a boil over medium-high heat. Lower the heat and simmer the stock for 2 hours. Skim the stock occasionally as it cooks.

4. Add the onion, leek, carrots, and celery to the same roasting pan used for the bones, and cook in the oven for 30 minutes, or until the vegetables are browned.

5. Add the 2 cups water, deglaze the roasting pan, scraping up all the bits from the bottom of the pan, and add everything to the soup pot. Add the bay leaves and parsley sprigs, and simmer the stock over medium-low heat for an additional 2 hours. Skim the stock occasionally as it cooks.

6. Strain the stock and cool quickly. Refrigerate the stock, covered, until needed. Plan to use within 2 days or freeze.

MAKES APPROXIMATELY 1½ TO 2 QUARTS

Fresh Tomato Sauce

2 tablespoons extra-virgin
  olive oil
2 cups diced onions
1 cup diced carrots
2 cups sliced washed
  mushrooms
1 tablespoon chopped
  garlic
4 cups peeled, seeded, and
  chopped plum tomatoes

2 tablespoons tomato paste
1 cup chicken stock
3 tablespoons chopped
  fresh basil
2 tablespoons chopped
  fresh parsley
Salt and freshly ground
  pepper to taste
1 to 2 tablespoons sugar
  (optional)

1. In a heavy saucepan, heat the oil over medium heat. Add the onions and carrots and cook until golden brown, 8 to 10 minutes, stirring often. Add the mushrooms and garlic and cook another 3 to 5 minutes.

2. Add the chopped tomatoes, tomato paste, and chicken stock and simmer over low heat for about 30 minutes, stirring occasionally. Add the basil and parsley and simmer for 15 minutes.

3. Puree the sauce in batches in a blender or food processor. Season with salt and freshly ground pepper and with sugar to taste, if needed.

MAKES JUST OVER 1 QUART

SPICY REMOULADE SAUCE

I recommend serving this sauce with Panfried Chicken and Maine Crab Cakes (page 80) and Panfried Herb-Crusted Flounder Fillets (page 97). Although this sauce is not typically Shaker, I think it goes so well with so many dishes that I had to include it.

2 cups mayonnaise
1 tablespoon capers,
  drained
2 tablespoons sweet pickle
  relish, drained
1 teaspoon anchovy paste
1 teaspoon minced garlic
2 teaspoons minced
  shallots
1 tablespoon minced
  scallions or chives

1 tablespoon chopped
  fresh parsley
1 teaspoon Worcestershire
  sauce
3 to 5 drops hot pepper
  sauce or ⅛ teaspoon
  cayenne pepper
Salt and freshly ground
  pepper to taste

In a large bowl, combine all of the ingredients and mix until well blended. Refrigerate, covered, until needed, up to 5 days.

MAKES APPROXIMATELY 2½ CUPS

TARTAR SAUCE

Freshly made tartar sauce is far superior to the commercial varieties. I recommend serving this sauce with the Panfried Chicken and Maine Crab Cakes (page 80), Peppered Bluefish Potato Cakes (page 102), and your favorite fried seafood.

2 cups mayonnaise
½ cup sweet pickle relish,
  drained
1 tablespoon capers,
  drained and chopped
2 teaspoons chopped
  shallots
1 teaspoon chopped garlic

2 teaspoons Dijon mustard
1 teaspoon Worcestershire
  sauce
1 teaspoon fresh lemon
  juice
1 to 2 drops hot pepper
  sauce or a pinch of
  cayenne pepper

| 1 tablespoon chopped fresh parsley | Salt and freshly ground pepper to taste |

In a large bowl, combine all of the ingredients and mix until well blended. Refrigerate, covered, until needed, up to 5 days.

MAKES APPROXIMATELY 2½ CUPS

CHUNKY APPLESAUCE

Apples were a large part of the Canterbury Shakers' livelihood in the early days. They maintained several fruit orchards and grew more than fifty varieties of apples alone. Apples were harvested, graded, and sold. The less attractive apples were made into the Shakers' famous applesauce. The Shakers also dried apples to be used during seasons when fresh were unavailable. The dried apples were used in cakes, muffins, stuffings, and even to make applesauce.

Today the Village maintains a single orchard of approximately 150 trees producing sixteen varieties of apples, such as Canadian Reds, Winesaps, Maiden Blush, Tolman Sweet, 20 Ounce, Dutchess of Oldinberg, and Gravenstein.

Shaker applesauce was traditionally made with boiled cider. In my recipe that follows, I substitute locally produced hard apple cider for the boiled cider for a very special applesauce.

| 5 pounds Granny Smith or Gravenstein apples | 1½ cups hard apple cider (see Sources) |
| ¼ cup sugar | |

1. Peel, core, and cube the apples.
2. In a large heavy saucepan, combine the apples, sugar, and hard cider. Cook over medium-low heat, stirring often, for about 20 to 30 minutes, or until the apples are soft. Stir vigorously to mash the apples.
3. The applesauce may be served warm, or cooled completely and refrigerated, tightly covered, up to 5 days.

MAKES APPROXIMATELY 3 PINTS

SPICY FRIED APPLES

Eldress Bertha taught me how to use cinnamon Red Hots in savory apple dishes to lend an appealing flavor and color.

I like to serve the apples with Shaker Sage Cakes (page 44) and Applewood Smoked Loin of Pork (page 54), by far my all-time favorite meal.

8 medium Granny Smith, Jonathan, or Gravenstein apples
½ cup (1 stick) unsalted butter

3 tablespoons Red Hots cinnamon candies
Sugar to taste (optional)

1. Peel, core, and cut each apple into 8 slices.
2. In a large frying pan, melt the butter over medium heat. Add the apple slices and sauté until they start to become translucent, about 5 minutes. Add the candy, tossing well. The candies will dissolve and turn the apples a pinkish-red color.
3. Season the apples with sugar, if desired, and serve warm.

SERVES 8

VANILLA DESSERT SAUCE

This is the most basic and versatile of the dessert sauces. It can also be used as the base for wonderful ice creams. The consistency of the sauce is determined by the amount of egg yolks used: the more yolks, the thicker the final sauce.

The chilled sauce may be flavored with additions such as fruit purees, extracts, liqueurs, nuts, and chocolate, to name a few.

1 cup milk
1 cup heavy cream

½ cup sugar, divided
4 to 6 egg yolks

1. In a heavy saucepan, combine the milk, cream, and ¼ cup sugar, and scald over medium-high heat. Remove from the heat and cool for 15 minutes.

2. In a large metal bowl, combine the egg yolks and the remaining ¼ cup sugar and whisk until pale yellow. Slowly stir in the scalded cream mixture.

3. Place the metal bowl over a double boiler on low heat. Cook, stirring constantly, until the mixture thickens and coats the back of a spoon, approximately 5 to 7 minutes. Strain and cool the sauce quickly. Refrigerate, covered, up to 3 days.

MAKES APPROXIMATELY 2½ CUPS

VARIATIONS

For Maple Pecan Vanilla Sauce: Substitute maple sugar (see Sources) for the sugar and add ½ cup finely chopped pecans at the end.

For Vanilla Fruit Sauce: Add approximately ⅓ cup pureed fruit, such as berries or peaches, at the end.

BITTERSWEET CHOCOLATE SAUCE

A simple dessert, such as Old-Fashioned Vanilla Bean Ice Cream (page 145), can be transformed into a sinfully delicious treat with the addition of homemade chocolate sauce.

The success of this recipe depends on the quality of chocolate used, so seek out the best bittersweet chocolate you can find.

1 pound bittersweet chocolate   **1 cup light cream**

1. Carefully chop the chocolate into small pieces and place in a large metal bowl.

2. In a saucepan, heat the cream just until boiling, then pour the hot cream over the chocolate and stir.

3. Place the bowl onto a double boiler over low heat, and stir until all the chocolate is melted and the sauce is smooth. Serve warm or refrigerate, covered, up to 5 days.

MAKES 2½ CUPS

CARAMEL SAUCE

The Shakers used to make a version of this called brown sugar sauce made with—you guessed it—brown sugar instead of granulated. Try swirling some into Old-Fashioned Vanilla Bean Ice Cream (page 145) during the freezing process.

¾ cup heavy cream
2 tablespoons (¼ stick)
   unsalted butter
1 cup sugar

¼ teaspoon fresh lemon
   juice
2 tablespoons water

1. In a saucepan, combine the cream and butter, and cook over low heat until the butter is melted.

2. In a heavy saucepan, combine the sugar, lemon juice, and water and cook over medium heat, stirring occasionally. Cook until the syrup is a medium golden brown, approximately 300°F. on a candy thermometer, watching carefully that the sugar doesn't burn. Remove from the heat immediately.

3. Carefully add the cream mixture, stirring until well blended. Be careful of splattering. Serve the sauce warm or cool, or refrigerate, covered, until needed, up to 5 days. To reheat the sauce, cook over low heat, stirring until melted.

MAKES APPROXIMATELY 1½ CUPS

OLD-FASHIONED
LARD PIECRUST

Sister Ethel swore that pie dough made with top-quality lard produces the best crust, very tender and flaky. I use a blend of 50 percent lard and 50 percent unsalted butter in my recipe.

1 cup pastry flour or
   unbleached all-purpose
   flour
¼ teaspoon salt
1 tablespoon sugar

3 tablespoons top-quality
   lard, chilled
3 tablespoons unsalted
   butter, chilled
¼ cup cold heavy cream or
   ice water

1. In a large bowl or the bowl of a food processor, combine the flour, salt, and sugar. Cut the lard and butter into the flour until it resembles coarse meal. Add the cream gradually and mix just until the dough comes together and forms a ball.

2. Lightly knead the dough until smooth and refrigerate, well wrapped, until needed, at least 30 minutes.

MAKES ONE 9-INCH PIE SHELL

VARIATION

For Coconut Pie Dough: Add 2 tablespoons unsweetened shredded coconut when you add the flour.

SISTER LEONA'S PIECRUSTS

SOUR MILK PIECRUST

5 cups sifted flour

1 tsp. salt

a pinch of soda

1 cup melted lard (creamy)

1 cup sour milk, warmed

—Combine the flour, salt and soda.

—Mix in the melted lard and milk.

—Mix just until the dough comes together.

HOT WATER PIECRUST

3 cups sifted flour

2 tsp. baking powder

a pinch of salt

1 cup lard

½ cup boiling water

—Combine the flour, baking powder and salt and cut the lard into the flour, course meal.

—Add the boiling water and mix until the dough comes together.

FLAKY PIE CRUST

2 cups pastry flour
2 tablespoons sugar
½ teaspoon salt

1 cup (2 sticks) chilled
   unsalted butter, cut into
   small pieces
9 tablespoons cold
   buttermilk

In a large bowl or food processor bowl combine the flour, sugar, and salt. Pulse or stir to blend. Add the butter and cut into the flour mixture until it resembles a coarse meal. Add the buttermilk and mix just until the dough comes together. (The dough may be refrigerated until needed, up to 3 days.)

MAKES 3 SINGLE-CRUST 10-INCH DEEP-DISH PIES

SYRUP OF COFFEE

This preparation is of great use to those who have long journeys to make. Take half a lb. of the best ground coffee, put into a sauce-pan containing three pints of water; when thoroughly steeped, pour off into another clean vessel and boil again until reduced to one pint. As it boils, add white sugar enough to give it the consistency of syrup. Take it from the fire; when cold, put into a bottle and seal. When traveling, if you wish for a cup of good coffee, you have only to put two or three teaspoonfuls of the syrup into an ordinary cup, then pour boiling water upon it, and it is ready for use. We have proved it to be good.

THE SHAKER MANIFESTO   SEPTEMBER 1878

AGRICULTURAL

Our Greely Mohawk Grape *has been the wonder of many this season, in earliness and quality. It was ripe fully two weeks ahead of the* Concord; *and though not so noble in form of bunches as this latter, is valuable as a predecessor. The Monarch Strawberry proved fully equal in size to reports; but there was an unequal ripening about it, that hurts its reputation somewhat.*

THE SHAKER MANIFESTO   NOVEMBER 1878

OHIO SHAKERS' SPICED GRAPE DRINK

Concord grape juice infused with cinnamon, cloves, and allspice and served over cracked ice has become our most popular beverage at The Creamery. This is also one of our most requested recipes.

2 quarts Concord grape
   juice
½ cup sugar
12 whole cloves
2 four-inch cinnamon
   sticks

3 tablespoons whole
   allspice
8 thin lemon slices for
   garnish

1. Combine all of the ingredients, except the lemon slices, in a large saucepot. Heat to a low simmer and cook for 20 to 30 minutes.

2. Strain the juice through a cheesecloth, discarding the spices, and chill well. Refrigerate, covered, until serving, up to 5 days. Serve in tall glasses over cracked ice garnished with a thin lemon slice.

SERVES 8

SOURCES

Being a true food enthusiast, I think finding the food is just as much fun as preparing the meal itself. In my cooking I always try to seek out local ingredients since they are often the freshest and of the highest quality. I enjoy knowing the farmers, gardeners, millers, and smokehouses who provide the foundations on which my cooking is built.

After every dinner two questions are frequently asked by at least one of the dinner guests, "Could I have the recipe for . . . ?" and "Where might I be able to find . . . ?" It would be pointless for me to include several of the recipes in this book without also including information on where several necessary ingredients can be obtained.

A special "thank you" to all of the old-time New England producers who help keep Shaker cooking alive and well.

American Spoon Foods
411 E. Lake Street
Petoskey, MI 49770
(800) 222-5886
Butternuts

Apple Mountain Cidre Works
Gould Hill Road
Contoocook, NH 03229
(603) 746-3811
Fresh apples and hard apple cider

Cabot Farmers' Cooperative
Creamery
Main Street, Box 128

Cabot, VT 05647
(802) 563-2231
Several types of Vermont Cheddar cheese and butter

Canterbury Shaker Village
288 Shaker Road
Canterbury, NH 03224
(603) 783-9511
Blueberry lavender vinegar, rose water, and dried culinary herbs

Ducktrap River Fish Farms
RFD 2, Box 378
Lincolnville, ME 04849

(207) 763-3960
*Northern fruitwood-
smoked seafood*

Flanders Bean-Hole-Bean Co.
P.O. Box 374
Epsom, New Hampshire 03234
(603) 435-8375
*Consultants for nonprofit
organizations*

Gray's Grist Mill
P.O. Box 422
Adamsville, RI 02801
(508) 636-6075
*Stone-ground flours, jonny cake
meal, brown bread flour mix,
three-grain pancake mix, and
boiled cider*

Luhr Jenson & Son, Inc.
P.O. Box 297
Hood River, OR 97031
(800) 535-1711
*Makers of Little Chief brand home
smokers*

Margie's Naturally Raised Veal
RFD 1, Box 436
Northwood, NH 03261
(603) 942-5427
*Naturally raised veal available in
retail and commercial cuts*

Nashoba Valley Winery
100 Wattaquadoc Hill Road
Bolton, MA 01740
(508) 779-5521
*Exceptional New England fruit
wines*

Nichols Garden Nursery
1190 N. Pacific Highway
Albany, OR 97321
Chocolate mint; free catalog

Nodine's Smokehouse
P.O. Box 1787
Torrington, CT 06790

(800) 222-2059
*Lightly hickory- and fruitwood-
smoked meats, fish, cheese, and
sausages*

North Family Farms
341 Shaker Road
Canterbury, NH 03224
(603) 783-4712
Maple products

Olde House Smoke House
335 Brier Bush Road
Canterbury, NH 03224
(603) 783-4405
*Oak-smoked meats, cheeses, and
sausages—custom smoking
available*

Salmon Falls Stoneware
P.O. Box 452
Dover, NH 03820
(603) 749-1467
*American salt-glazed pottery—
including bean pots*

Sandy Mush Herb Nursery
Route 2, Surrett Cove Road
Leicester, NC 28748
Chocolate mint; catalog $4.00

Sunnyside Maples
Route 106
Loudon, NH 03301
(603) 783-9961
Maple products

William's Smoke House
P.O. Box 1543
Bennington, VT 05201
(802) 442-1000
*Corncob-smoked meats, fish,
cheese, and sausages*

Wills Wood's Boiled Cider
RFD 2
Springfield, VT 05156
(802) 263-5547
New England boiled cider

SHAKER MUSEUMS

Canterbury Shaker Village
288 Shaker Road
Canterbury, NH 03224
(603) 783-9511

Fruitlands Museum
102 Prospect Hill Road
Harvard, MA 01451
(508) 456-3924

Hancock Shaker Village
P.O. Box 898
Pittsfield, MA 01202
(413) 443-0188

Mount Lebanon Shaker Village
Shaker Road, P.O. Box 628
New Lebanon, NY 12125
(518) 794-9500

Museum at Lower Shaker
  Village
P.O. Box 25, Route 4A
Enfield, NH 03748
(603) 632-5533

Shaker Heritage Society Trustee's Office
1848 Shaker Meeting House
Albany-Shaker Road
Albany, NY 12211
(518) 456-7890

Shaker Historical Society
16740 South Park Boulevard
Shaker Heights, OH 44120
(216) 921-1201

The Shaker Museum
Shaker Museum Road
Old Chatham, NY 12136
(518) 794-9100

The Shaker Museum at Sabbathday Lake
RFD 1, Box 640
Poland Springs, ME 04274
(207) 926-4597

Shakertown at Pleasant Hill, Kentucky
3500 Lexington Road
Harrodsburg, KY 40330
(608) 734-5411

BIBLIOGRAPHY

Haller, James, and Jeffrey Paige. *Cooking in the Shaker Spirit.* Yankee Books, Camden, Maine, 1990.

Lindsay, Bertha. *Seasoned with Grace.* The Countryman Press, Woodstock, Vermont, 1987.

Miller, Amy Bess Williams, and Persis Fuller. *The Best of Shaker Cooking.* Macmillan Publishing Company, New York, 1985.

INDEX

Conversion Chart

EQUIVALENT IMPERIAL AND METRIC MEASUREMENTS

American cooks use standard containers, the 8-ounce cup and a tablespoon that takes exactly 16 level fillings to fill that cup level. Measuring by cup makes it very difficult to give weight equivalents, as a cup of densely packed butter will weigh considerably more than a cup of flour. The easiest way therefore to deal with cup measurements in recipes is to take the amount by volume rather than by weight. Thus the equation reads:

1 cup = 240 ml = 8 fl. oz.
$\frac{1}{2}$ cup = 120 ml = 4 fl. oz.

It is possible to buy a set of American cup measures in major stores around the world.

In the States, butter is often measured in sticks. One stick is the equivalent of 8 tablespoons. One tablespoon of butter is therefore the equivalent to $\frac{1}{2}$ ounce/15 grams.

LIQUID MEASURES

Fluid Ounces	U.S. Measures	Imperial Measures	Milliliters
	1 TSP	1 TSP	5
$\frac{1}{4}$	2 TSP	1 Dessertspoon	7
$\frac{1}{2}$	1 TBS	1 TBS	15
1	2 TBS	2 TBS	28
2	$\frac{1}{4}$ CUP	4 TBS	56
4	$\frac{1}{2}$ CUP OR $\frac{1}{4}$ PINT		110
5		$\frac{1}{4}$ PINT OR 1 GILL	140
6	$\frac{3}{4}$ CUP		170
8	1 CUP OR $\frac{1}{2}$ PINT		225
9			250, $\frac{1}{4}$ LITER
10	1 $\frac{1}{4}$ CUPS	$\frac{1}{2}$ PINT	280
12	1 $\frac{1}{2}$ CUPS OR $\frac{3}{4}$ PINT		340
15		$\frac{3}{4}$ PINT	420
16	2 CUPS OR 1 PINT		450

SOLID MEASURES

U.S. and Imperial Measures		Metric Measures	
Ounces	Pounds	Grams	Kilos
1		28	
2		56	
3 $\frac{1}{2}$		100	
4	$\frac{1}{4}$	112	
5		140	
6		168	
8	$\frac{1}{2}$	225	
9		250	$\frac{1}{4}$
12	$\frac{3}{4}$	340	
16	1	450	

U.S. and Imperial Measures		Metric Measures	
Ounces	Pounds	Grams	Kilos
18		500	$\frac{1}{2}$
20	1 $\frac{1}{4}$	560	
24	1 $\frac{1}{2}$	675	
27		750	$\frac{3}{4}$

SUGGESTED EQUIVALENTS AND SUBSTITUTES FOR INGREDIENTS

all-purpose flour—plain flour
arugula—rocket
beet—beetroot
confectioner's sugar—icing sugar
cornstarch—cornflour
eggplant—aubergine
granulated sugar—caster sugar
kielbasa—Polish sausage
lima beans—broad beans
pearl onions—pickling onions
scallion—spring onion
shortening—white fat
snow pea—mangetout
sour cherry—morello cherry
squab—poussin
squash—courgettes or marrow
unbleached flour—strong, white flour
vanilla bean—vanilla pod
zest—rind
zucchini—courgettes
light cream—single cream
heavy cream—double cream
half and half—12% fat milk
buttermilk—ordinary milk
sour milk—add 1 tablespoon vinegar or lemon juice to 1 cup minus 1 tablespoon lukewarm milk. Let stand for 5 minutes.
cheesecloth—muslin

OVEN TEMPERATURE EQUIVALENTS

Fahrenheit	Celsius	Gas Mark	Description
225	110	$\frac{1}{4}$	Cool
250	130	$\frac{1}{2}$	
275	140	1	Very Slow
300	150	2	
325	170	3	Slow
350	180	4	Moderate
375	190	5	
400	200	6	Moderately Hot
425	220	7	Fairly Hot
450	230	8	Hot
475	240	9	Very Hot
500	250	10	Extremely Hot

Any broiling recipes can be used with the grill of the oven, but beware of high-temperature grills.